INDIANS

POCAHONTAS, *Seymour*
SACAGAWEA, *Seymour*
SEQUOYAH, *Snow*
SITTING BULL, *Stevenson*
SQUANTO, *Stevenson*
TECUMSEH, *Stevenson*

NAVAL HEROES

DAVID FARRAGUT, *Long*
GEORGE DEWEY, *Long*
JOHN PAUL JONES, *Snow*
MATTHEW CALBRAITH PERRY, *Scharbach*
OLIVER HAZARD PERRY, *Long*
RAPHAEL SEMMES, *Snow*
STEPHEN DECATUR, *Smith*

NOTED WIVES and MOTHERS

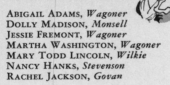

ABIGAIL ADAMS, *Wagoner*
DOLLY MADISON, *Monsell*
JESSIE FREMONT, *Wagoner*
MARTHA WASHINGTON, *Wagoner*
MARY TODD LINCOLN, *Wilkie*
NANCY HANKS, *Stevenson*
RACHEL JACKSON, *Govan*

SCIENTISTS and INVENTORS

ALBERT EINSTEIN, *Hammontree*
ALECK BELL, *Widdemer*
CYRUS MCCORMICK, *Dobler*
ELI WHITNEY, *Snow*
ELIAS HOWE, *Corcoran*
ELIZABETH BLACKWELL, *Henry*
GEORGE CARVER, *Stevenson*
GEORGE EASTMAN, *Henry*
HENRY FORD, *Aird and Ruddiman*
JOHN AUDUBON, *Mason*
LUTHER BURBANK, *Burt*
MARIA MITCHELL, *Melin*
ROBERT FULTON, *Henry*
SAMUEL MORSE, *Snow*
TOM EDISON, *Guthridge*
WALTER REED, *Higgins*
WILBUR AND ORVILLE WRIGHT, *Stevenson*
WILL AND CHARLIE MAYO, *Hammontree*

SOCIAL and CIVIC LEADERS

BETSY ROSS, *Weil*
[illegible] T. WASHINGTON,
[illegible]
[illegible]*n*
[illegible]*on*
[illegible]*Moore*
[illegible]*goner*
LILIUOKALANI, [illegible]*n*
LUCRETIA MOTT, *Burnett*
MOLLY PITCHER, *Stevenson*
OLIVER WENDELL HOLMES, JR., *Dunham*
SUSAN ANTHONY, *Monsell*

SOLDIERS

ANTHONY WAYNE, *Stevenson*
BEDFORD FORREST, *Parks*
DAN MORGAN, *Bryant*
ETHAN ALLEN, *Winders*
FRANCIS MARION, *Steele*
ISRAEL PUTNAM, *Stevenson*
JEB STUART, *Winders*
NATHANAEL GREENE, *Peckham*
ROBERT E. LEE, *Monsell*
SAM HOUSTON, *Stevenson*
TOM JACKSON, *Monsell*
U. S. GRANT, *Stevenson*
WILLIAM HENRY HARRISON, *Peckham*
ZACK TAYLOR, *Wilkie*

STATESMEN

ABE LINCOLN, *Stevenson*
ANDY JACKSON, *Stevenson*
DAN WEBSTER, *Smith*
FRANKLIN ROOSEVELT, *Weil*
HENRY CLAY, *Monsell*
JAMES MONROE, *Widdemer*
JEFF DAVIS, *de Grummond and Delaune*
JOHN MARSHALL, *Monsell*
TEDDY ROOSEVELT, *Parks*
WOODROW WILSON, *Monsell*

L   ott

Illustrated by Nathan Goldstein

Lucretia Mott

Girl of Old Nantucket

By Constance Buel Burnett

THE **BOBBS-MERRILL** COMPANY, INC.
A SUBSIDIARY OF HOWARD W. SAMS & CO., INC.
Publishers • INDIANAPOLIS • NEW YORK

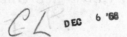

For
Penny and Kit and Robin
who, with all young Americans,
cherish
the ways of freedom.

Illustrations

Full pages

Numerous smaller illustrations

Contents

CHILDHOOD OF FAMOUS AMERICANS

LUCRETIA MOTT: GIRL OF OLD NANTUCKET

★ # Lucretia Mott

Girl of Old Nantucket

Mush for Breakfast

EARLY ONE morning in the year 1800 a noisy March wind played over the island of Nantucket. It whistled around the corners of the gray, shingled houses. It rattled the shutters. One of these big square houses on Fair Street belonged to Thomas Coffin, a Quaker sea captain.

Inside, little Lucretia Coffin stirred in her sleep once. Then she sat up, her black eyes wide-open and bright. Lucretia always woke up quickly and completely, as soon as she was roused. Beside her in the four-poster bed, her older sister Sally lay curled up like a caterpillar. Her nose was buried in the patchwork quilt.

11

"Thee sleeps so hard, Sally." Lucretia nudged the mound under the quilt. "Wake up, lazy! If we get our chores done before breakfast, Mother said we could go down to the wharves to see her off. I'm going to do mine."

Lucretia hopped out of the warm bed onto the chilly floor. She wriggled out of her nightgown and began to put on her clothes. In a minute she was buttoning her gray homespun dress.

Sally stretched and yawned. She shivered as a sudden gust shook the shutters again. "That horrid wind!" she complained. "Always blowing sand into the house and giving us more dusting to do! We've dusted and swept the same sand out of the house a hundred times."

"It's not horrid. It's a good, strong wind," Lucretia argued. "If it weren't for the wind, the whaling ships couldn't sail out of Nantucket Harbor. Father's ship would never reach China. Then there would be no whale oil on Nantucket,

12

and no China goods for Mother to sell in her shop. Without the wind we Islanders would be as poor as castaways."

"Who told thee so?" Sally mumbled sleepily. She pulled her petticoat over her head and reached for her shoes.

"Father. He told me that people on an island have to be brave sailors. That's why we Nantucket children learn to read the compass. So we know the points of the compass by heart and can tell the directions of the wind."

Two minutes later the little girls were hard at work dusting the "Great Room." It stretched from the front of the house to the back. Sally was big and strong. She cleaned the floors and tidied the hearth. Lucretia carefully dusted all the ladder-backed chairs.

Most important of all, she climbed on the settle by the fireplace to dust the mantelpiece. On it lay the family telescope. Lucretia polished the lens carefully every day with a piece of soft India silk. It must be kept unscratched and clean, so they might recognize Father's ship as soon as it appeared on the horizon.

Next, the two of them went into the small room across the hall. Here Mother kept shop. Sally took the heavy bolts of nankeen cloth and the rolls of China silk off the shelves. She dusted underneath. Lucretia had deft and careful hands. She wiped the packages of spice, cinnamon and ginger. They were wrapped in thin Chinese paper colored bright-red and canary-yellow. She dusted the small tin boxes of China and India tea and the blue and white dishes. Father had brought this chinaware back from Canton.

"I hear Mother in the kitchen," said Sally. She shook and folded a length of silk. "And here comes that lazy Thomas! What a racket he makes! You'd think by the sound that he was doing all the work around here."

14

A boy's heavy boots clattered downstairs. "Hello," called Thomas, as he poked his head into the shop. "I'll wager I can tell how the wind's blowing without any weather vane."

Thomas took pride in telling the family what the weather was each day. It was his special duty when Captain Coffin was away at sea. He pushed back the bolt, opened the front door and sniffed the air which blew into the room.

"Phew!" He made a wry face. "Smell the whale oil from the harbor! Wind's north by east, and a spanking breeze it is. Mother," he shouted down the stairs to the cellar kitchen, "thee'll get to the Continent quickly today!" People on Nantucket Island always called Cape Cod the Continent.

"No need to tell the whole village, Thomas," Mother called back. "Thy voice is louder than Jerry's fish horn. Come to breakfast, children. Betsy and I have already eaten."

Mother was going on a trading journey to the mainland. She had many things to do before the boat left at midday. Everyone had to help. Her brisk voice told the children she wanted no nonsense. They all knew they'd better do their share of the work quickly and well.

"Thomas, run out to the pump at the end of the lane." She handed him a pair of buckets. "Bring in six of these before thee goes to school. Now scud along, lad. Thee hasn't much time. Be sure thee gets enough fresh water every day."

Next Mother turned to Sally. She pointed to the kettle which hung in the big kitchen fire-place. All the cooking was done there. "Take the kettle off the crane, Sally. The water is hot enough now to wash the breakfast dishes."

When Mother went trading on the Continent she was gone three days at least. She always cooked enough clam and fish chowder to last the family till she got home.

16

"Set the skillet of salt pork away from the flames, child," she warned Lucretia. "That's it. Let it simmer on the hot hearth. Mind the spitting fat! It may jump on Elizabeth."

"Not so close, Betsy darling." Lucretia pushed her two-year-old sister gently away from the fire-place. "Oh, Mother," she begged eagerly, "why can't Betsy stay home this time instead of going to Grandmother's? I promise not to let her out of my sight one minute. She always minds me. The time when you're gone always seems so long. It would be so much more fun if Betsy was here with us. Please let her stay."

"Well, I never, Lucretia Coffin!" Sally turned so quickly she almost upset the dishpan. "Mother hasn't ever left Betsy with me, and I'm the old-est. Thee's only seven."

Sally was so provoked she forgot what she was doing. The wet cup she held was slippery and so were her fingers. There was a crash and a tinkle as the cup fell to the floor.

"Oh!" wailed Sally. She stopped to pick up the pieces. "It just slipped out of my hand as I was washing it!"

18

"Oh, dear," cried Lucretia in the same breath, "there goes the blue Canton cup Grandfather brought me from China! Thee *is* a clumsy!" Lucretia's black eyes flashed. "I can never replace that cup!"

"Serves thee right for not using thy pewter mug, like the rest of us," retorted Sally. "And look, Mother, she hasn't finished her mush again." Sally pointed to the half-empty bowl on the table. "No wonder she is small and thin. She never eats all her food!"

"Tattletale!" Lucretia stamped her foot.

"Spitfire!"

At the sound of their angry voices, little Elizabeth began to whimper. She ran to her mother.

"You see. Quarreling frightens her. How many times must I tell you that Quaker ways are the ways of peace? Is this an example to set a small sister?" Mother gathered up the baby and spoke sternly to Sally.

19

"For a girl of ten, Sally, thee is careless. Thee only half listens to directions. Yesterday thee came back from Cousin Macy's with a bobbin of black thread when I asked for white. Thy knitting has many dropped stitches. How can I be sure thee wouldn't be just as careless with Elizabeth? Thee must learn to pay attention."

"As for thee, Lucretia, one of the first lessons a Quaker child must learn is to control her temper. Thee cannot be trusted with Elizabeth until thee learns not to quarrel."

Mother put the baby in her high chair. Then she led Lucretia to a stool by the hearth. She picked up the big family Bible.

"Either finish every bit of thy mush, or learn by heart the fourth and fifth verses from the thirteenth chapter of First Corinthians. If thee can recite them without a mistake before the school bell rings thee may go. Otherwise thee must stay home."

20

Lucretia hated to miss school. She thought school was fun because she learned quickly. She looked at her mush and made a face. It was cold now. Besides, she had eaten all the molasses.

"I'll learn the Bible verses," she decided.

"Very well," Mother said quietly. She glanced at the kitchen clock. "Thee has just ten minutes. 'Tis a pity thee didn't choose to eat thy mush. There will be nothing else for thy breakfast for quite a while."

"How long?" asked Lucretia anxiously.

"Until thee learns to like it," answered Mother. "Who ever heard of a Nantucket child being finicky about food! A sailor's daughter eats everything."

"Yes siree," agreed Thomas. He had just come in with two buckets full of water. "Sailors have to eat hardtack and whale blubber. Grandfather Folger told me once he ate grasshoppers when he went to Arabia."

Lucretia shivered in disgust. She bent over the Bible Mother had placed in her lap. "Charity suffereth long, and is kind." She began studying the fourth verse. It did not take her long to learn all of it.

Soon she was able to start on the fifth verse. By the time Sally had finished the dishes and Mother had swept the kitchen and Thomas had brought in two more buckets of water, Lucretia knew both verses. She recited them for Mother without a mistake.

"Now I can go to school," she cried joyfully. "And guess what?" She threw her arms around Mother in a quick, short hug. "I like mush now, so thee needn't cook it so often."

"Oho," laughed Mother. "Time enough to prove that when I get home!"

Mother's Trip to Cape Cod

THOMAS, SALLY and Lucretia sat on the front stoop. Beside them were the bundles they were going to carry to the boat for Mother.

It was a little after eleven o'clock, and the morning session of school had been let out. The Coffin children had been excused for the rest of the day since their mother needed them. The family had eaten a quick lunch of cornbread and buttermilk. All the tasks that needed to be done before Mother left had been finished.

Mother was locking up her shop while the Coffin family waited for Grandmother and Grandfather Folger to come after Elizabeth.

"Why don't we all stay at Grandmother's while Mother's away? I wish we could." Sally sighed. "There are always plenty of people there. I like being on the hill above the village. I can see almost clear across the island. And there are lambs to play with on the commons. I wonder why they call those fields up there the commons instead of giving them a regular name."

"It's because they're common property," said Thomas. "They belong to everyone."

Someday she was going to know as much as Thomas, Lucretia decided. She had noticed that boys knew lots of useful things. And when she was thirteen, like Thomas, she wouldn't be at the bottom of the spelling class either.

"Every family has a right to graze sheep on the commons," Thomas went on. "But they mustn't get mixed up. We know our sheep because they have two V-shaped notches on their ears. All the sheep there are marked."

24

Lucretia opened her eyes wide. It was really surprising how much Thomas knew. "Were they born that way?"

"No, silly!" Thomas laughed. "It's done with a knife, but it doesn't hurt. If the sheep weren't marked no one would be able to find his own at shearingtime. I've watched Father slit the ears of our sheep."

"I love shearingtime," said Sally. "I wish it were here again. There'll be dancing and feasting on the commons. And Father's boat will have come back from India—he promised us."

Thomas stood up suddenly. He almost knocked Sally off the steps in his hurry to run down the street. "Here's Grandfather's calash!" he shouted to Mother. A two-wheeled carriage was coming around the corner of Fair Street.

Captain Folger called whoa to his horse in front of the stoop. Just then Mother came out with the baby in her arms.

Grandmother leaned out to take Elizabeth. "We'll not stay and talk, Anna," she told Mother. "It will only delay thee getting to the boat. But we could use either Lucretia or Sally, if thee can spare one of them from home tasks. Our ewes are lambing already. Thee knows an extra pair of hands in the house is always welcome at such a time."

"Aye—and there's a place here amidships for a pair of smart young legs too—legs that can run errands." Grandfather pointed invitingly to the space between Grandmother and himself. "We've three newborn lambs in the shed right now," he added.

"Oh," cried Lucretia, "I love baby lambs, and I haven't seen any for a year. How I'd love to see them and play with them!"

"Oh," Sally wailed, "so would I!"

"There!" thought Lucretia. "She's going to say she's the oldest, so she can go."

Sally dug her toe into the sand by the big carriage wheel. Sure enough, Lucretia heard her say in a very small voice, "I'm the oldest. I——" Poor Sally took a deep breath and finished quite differently from what Lucretia expected. "I guess I ought to stay home and help Thomas mind the house. Let Lucretia go this time. She can help Grandmother and see the lambs too."

Lucretia had opened her mouth to say something sharp. Now her face grew pink with shame. She knew the real reason Sally wanted to go to Grandmother's. It was because she was afraid to be alone in the house while Mother was away.

When the girls went to bed after dark, Lucretia always went ahead with the candle. Lucretia never imagined things were any different at night from the way they were in the daytime. Sally thought she saw goblins in every dark corner. If Sally were left alone tonight in the four-poster bed, she wouldn't sleep a wink!

"You go, Sally," Lucretia offered generously. "Mother said we could roast potatoes tonight in the fireplace ashes. And you know—I—I like potatoes very much."

"That settles everything," Captain Folger's cheerful voice boomed above them from the hood of the calash. "Hoist Sally up over the wheel, Thomas, and we'll get under way."

Lucretia thought potatoes a rare treat. Nothing grew well in the sandy soil of Nantucket island. Potatoes were saved for special occasions. But, just the same, newborn lambs came only once a year! Lucretia gave a deep sigh as Grandfather slapped the reins across old Dennis' flanks. The calash soon disappeared.

"And now," said Mother, turning back into the house, "we must hurry. Get thy bonnet and pelisse, Lucretia. It will be colder down by the harbor than it is here. Thee must not get sick while I am away."

The bonnet and wrap were on a wooden peg in the room she and Sally shared. When Lucretia came down with them, Mother was sorting the bundles on the stoop.

"Thee may carry the carded wool, Lucretia. It's not heavy. Thomas, take the two packages of Nantucket candles, and don't drop them. They are worth everything else I'm taking."

Mother picked up her carpetbag, her umbrella and a large basket of cranberry preserves.

"Now we're off," she said cheerfully. "If I make a good trade who knows but I'll bring home a few pennies' worth of toffee or mint drops?" She started briskly down the street.

"Sweets—oh, goody!" Lucretia's short legs gave an extra skip. Her poke bonnet bobbed up and down as she hurried along between her tall mother and Thomas. Her tongue kept time with her feet. Mother's trading journeys always started Lucretia asking questions.

"Nantucket candles are the very best, aren't they?" she asked with pride.

"People are willing to pay more for them," said Mother. "That's why I take a supply when I go to the Continent."

"What makes them better?"

"They're made of spermaceti," Thomas informed Lucretia. "I'll wager you can't spell that, Miss Question Box."

"What's sper-ma-ceti?" Lucretia stumbled over the big word.

"Whale oil."

"Just any whale oil?" There were many kinds of whales, Lucretia knew.

"No."

"Then what kind?" Lucretia persisted.

Thomas thought it was fun to see how long he could keep Lucretia asking questions. He usually kept her going a long time.

"Sperm oil," answered Thomas shortly.

Mother couldn't help laughing. "Now, then, stop being such a tease, Thomas. When the oil from the sperm whale is boiled, Lucretia, a scum rises to the top——"

"Like the scum thee lets me spoon off jelly?"

"Something like that. Only this is a kind of wax, called spermaceti. Candles dipped in it burn brighter and longer than candles dipped in tallow. People are always glad to buy all I can bring to the Continent."

While they were talking they had been walking through the village, past many gray, shingled houses and white picket fences that looked much like Lucretia's own house and fence.

As they went by, Cousin Macy waved to them from her shop window that faced Main Street.

Great-aunt Gardiner was waiting for them in her doorway. She held up a snipping of gray tape. "If it's not too much trouble, Anna, match this as near as thee can. 'Twould be a real favor."

Cousin Hetty ran out of her house with a list and some money in a twist of brown paper. "I need pins more than anything else," she said to Mother, "but don't go out of thy way, Anna."

That was the way it was on the small island. People did things for one another, and almost everybody was related to everybody else. Mother said it made her mind easy when she went to the Continent. The children couldn't get into very serious trouble with so many relatives close by.

Now they were near the wharves. There was a thundering clatter in the air. It was the sound of oil barrels being rolled out of the whaling ships' holds. Mother and Thomas and Lucretia had to shout to one another. Lucretia looked up at the tangle of masts and rigging. It made a crisscross pattern against the sky.

They passed the blacksmith shops. There harpoons and spears for the whaling fleet were hammered into shape. The ring of the anvils went on from morning till night on the wharves of Nantucket. So did a steady pounding from the coopers' shops, where wooden oil barrels for the whaling fleet were made.

Mother's business this morning took her past the big wharves to a small dock. Captain Swain's packet boat, the "Seabird," waited there. It would take passengers across Nantucket Sound to the Cape Cod mainland.

Mother's bundles were soon stowed in the cabin. The "Seabird's" sails were hoisted. As the boat left the dock Mother called back over a lengthening stretch of water, "Lucretia, don't thee forget thy knitting. Thee should have sixty bouts done when I get home. Thomas, be sure not to leave the house at any time, unless thee knows the kitchen fire is out!"

The Tern

THE "SEABIRD" rounded the point and sailed out of Nantucket harbor. "Come on, I'm going to Obed's," Thomas said. Obed was a fisherman and their good friend. "He promised to show me how to whittle a ring out of whalebone. Thee can watch," he added grandly, as though he were doing Lucretia a favor.

"It's lots of fun at Obed's," agreed Lucretia eagerly. She decided to put off her knitting till evening. "I'll play with Noah the parrot. I wish we had a pet like Noah. Debbie Coleman's father brought her a parrot from South America. I wish we had one."

"I wish we had a parrot, too, but Mother won't hear of it. She had to live with Grandfather's parrot all those years. There's no use teasing her for one. You know she doesn't like parrots. We might ask for some other pet."

"Maybe Obed's finished those toy whaleboats he was making. Maybe he'll let me play with one," Lucretia said hopefully.

Thomas hooted at the idea. "He certainly won't! Why, they're not toys—they belong on his model of the 'Dolphin.'"

The children took a narrow, sandy footpath. It led along the water front, from the dock to the cabin where Obed lived. Thomas went ahead. As Lucretia followed she noticed some ragged, dirty boys throwing stones into the water. They were trying to hit a few sea gulls that were quarreling and pecking at one another.

"Look," she called. "Those Indian boys are bothering the sea gulls."

36

"It's nothing. The gulls are always scrapping over whale blubber. Sailors throw it overboard from the ships." Thomas did not even bother to turn his head. "Obed's dory is tied to his landing. He's home!" Thomas started to run.

"But, Thomas——" Lucretia called after him. She wanted to tell him that the boys were teasing the gulls. They were children of the poorest families on the island—Indian children.

There had been Indians on Nantucket long before her own ancestors had arrived, Father had told Lucretia. Once they had been fine, healthy people. It was the Indians who had taught the white men how to hunt whales off Nantucket beaches.

The Indian children ran wild along the shores and beaches. They were mischief-makers, and sometimes they were cruel to animals. Thomas knew this, but he didn't wait to see what they were doing.

The cries of the gulls stopped suddenly. When she looked back, Lucretia saw them flying off. She ran after Thomas.

Noah the parrot got very much excited whenever Obed had visitors. As Lucretia stepped into the cabin he jumped up and down on his perch. He gave a loud squawk. "Come in and shut up!" he greeted her.

"Don't mind him." His master laughed. "Noah gets mixed up. He means 'Come in and shut the door.' I'm mighty glad to see you both," Obed continued. "The 'Dolphin' is finished. Right pretty, isn't she?" He held up his handiwork for them to see.

"Oh," breathed Lucretia admiringly. "It's a beautiful ship."

Even Noah gave a shrill whistle as if he approved of Obed's work.

Thomas laughed. Thee said it right this time, Noah! Thee likes it too!"

38

Obed's little model was a perfect copy of a whaling bark. Her foremast and mainmast carried square sails. She was complete from bow to stern. The small wooden blocks on her rigging were no bigger than poppy seed. Her ropes were as fine as a spider's web. On her deck was a little furnace for boiling imaginary whale oil.

But most wonderful of all to Lucretia were the six tiny rowboats. They were stacked on the "Dolphin's" hatches. These were the whaleboats a ship like the "Dolphin" would send out to chase whales. Each had small oars and spears. Each had a harpoon, with its line coiled neatly in a tub.

"How did thee do it, Obed?" exclaimed Thomas. "How could thee do such fine work?"

The old man grinned with pleasure. His whaling days were over. He made a safer living now. He fished in Nantucket waters and built ship models. He whittled many useful things out of whalebone and made all of them beautiful.

No matter what Thomas said, Obed's ship models looked like toys to Lucretia. Some stood by his workbench and some on the mantel above his fireplace. Each was different. On some Obed had placed little wooden men. Lucretia went from one to another. She clasped her hands behind her back so she would not be tempted to touch anything.

She forgot all about the parrot until he called from his perch in the corner. "Come scratch my head, dearie," Noah coaxed.

Lucretia knew all Noah's tricks. The wicked old bird could coo as sweetly as a dove. He would pretend to fall asleep while she scratched his head gently. Then when he thought he had her well fooled, he would suddenly nip her fingers when she least expected it.

"Not this time. Thee won't catch me, bad Noah." Lucretia rubbed his head with a shaving from Obed's bench.

Thomas was a long time over his whittling lesson. Lucretia wandered to the window that looked out on the harbor. The Indian boys were still playing on the shore. One of them had waded into the water. He was pulling something in—a live creature which was struggling to get away. It looked like a bird.

Lucretia opened the door of the cabin to see. Then she was sure. The voices of the Indian children came to her plainly.

"Look out! It'll nip you!"

"Better kill it!"

"Naw," shouted a third. "Haul it in by its wing! It can't hurt you then!"

"Them things can peck your eyes out!"

"I'll get an oar. We can bang its head in."

Lucretia did not wait to call Thomas and Obed. She thought only of stopping the children in time. As she raced down the path, the boy threw the bird toward the beach.

In mid-air it tried to fly, then flopped on the sand. One wing was dragging. Now the boys made a circle around it. They poked it with sticks. The bird defended itself fiercely with its beak. It tried to fly.

The anger inside Lucretia made her feel as tall and strong as a giant. It gave speed to her flying feet. She reached the circle just as one boy brought up an oar.

Lucretia flung herself on him. "Stop it! I won't let thee!" She seized the oar and tried to wrench it out of his hand.

But the boy was twice her size. He brushed her aside easily. "Here you, leave off!" he said gruffly. "Get out of the way and leave us alone, or you'll get hurt."

Lucretia flung herself at him again. She hammered his chest with both her fists.

"Quit that!" he shouted. He raised the oar threateningly.

42

"Don't thee dare!" screamed Lucretia, still beating at him. But she felt small and helpless now. If only Thomas—— Then she suddenly noticed the Indian boy's bare feet. Lucretia stamped on them as hard as she could with her stout, buttoned shoes. This was a form of attack that the boy had not expected.

"Ouch!" He let go of the oar to clutch his foot. Two other boys grabbed Lucretia. As she twisted and pulled to get free, they all tripped on the fallen oar. They went down together.

Obed and Thomas had heard Lucretia's cries. Now they came running out of the cabin.

"Off with you!" roared Obed at the boys. "Get away from here!" Seeing a man, they scurried away like crabs.

"How did you run afoul of those rowdies?" Obed wanted to know. He brushed Lucretia off. Her bonnet dangled from one string. Her hair was tousled and her face smudged.

"The gull——" Lucretia panted. She forgot her dirty pelisse and damaged bonnet, though Mother would certainly eye them sternly. She forgot even to thank Obed. She just ran as fast as she could to where Thomas already knelt on the sand, holding the bird.

Obed followed. He stooped and gently examined the injured bird.

"It's a tern, not a gull," said Thomas. He pointed to its slender wings and small body.

"Don't try to pick him up. His wing is broken," Obed warned Thomas. The tern had lunged at the boy's hand. "I've a better idea. I'll be back in a minute."

Obed went and got a blanket. They trapped the helpless creature in its folds. Then they carried him gently to the old whaler's cabin. There they laid him in a large fish basket made of beach grass. The bird was quiet from exhaustion or pain and made no attempt to move.

"Leave him be quiet," Obed advised. "If he's given a chance that wing may mend. Trouble with wild things is, their own kind kills 'em when they're hurt—if the boys don't."

"That must have been what the big white gulls were trying to do in the water. They were pecking at him," Lucretia said indignantly.

Noah noticed all the attention the tern was getting. Thomas and Lucretia hung over the basket. Noak liked to be the center of interest himself. So he began to show off his tricks, one after another. First he rattled his feed cup. Next he tried to sing in a cracked voice. Then he turned somersaults on his perch. When no one looked at him, he became angry.

"Buzzard!" he screeched at the tern. He added a string of insulting names. Noah had learned these during a long life at sea.

Obed hurled a soft rag at him that he used for polishing whalebone.

"Pipe down!" he commanded sternly. Then he grinned. "He's jealous," he explained to Lucretia and Thomas. "If that critter—" he motioned toward the tern— "stays here long, I expect Noah will work himself into a fit. I've known parrots to get sick from jealousy."

Lucretia and Thomas looked at each other. They were both thinking the same thing.

"If thee doesn't want the tern, Obed," Thomas blurted out, "we do. Maybe thee would lend us this basket. We'll bring it back."

"We could carry the tern home in it," Lucretia explained eagerly. "And we could have him for a pet. Just think . . ." She jumped to her feet and clapped her hands. "We've never had a pet!"

"You're welcome to basket and bird." Obed chuckled. "I've got all I can take care of, and Noah won't have him here. Better take this too." He fetched an old piece of sailcloth from the shed where he kept his fishing nets.

"Your pet may try to jump out on the way. He'll be scared crazy if you don't cover him up with something," Obed warned.

"Oh, Obed, thank thee!" chorused Thomas and Lucretia.

"Thank thee, thank thee," Noah mimicked from his perch. "Good riddance too," he muttered to himself. He burst into ear-splitting laughter.

That evening Lucretia sat down beside Thomas on the kitchen floor in front of a bright fire. Her knitting needles flashed busily in and out of the stocking she was making. Her brother was whittling a large spoon which he intended to give to his mother.

Near her in his basket dozed Sinbad the tern. They had thought of the name for him on the way home. He seemed contented to stay in the basket. He had even pecked hungrily at some moist bread they had placed beside him.

However, he wouldn't touch any food when he thought they were looking at him. He wouldn't allow either one of them to come near enough to him to touch him.

"I wonder if Mother will like him," Lucretia said. "Do you think she will allow us to keep him in a cage?"

"I don't think she'll let us keep him in the house," Thomas said. "She'd be much more apt to let us have him if he's already outside."

"But how can we keep him safe outdoors when he's hurt?" Lucretia cried.

"Tomorrow," said Thomas, "we'll have to think where we can keep him outside. Mother won't want him in the house."

"Sinbad's much nicer than a parrot. I'm glad now we haven't got one." Lucretia yawned sleepily. She was glad too that she hadn't gone to Grandfather Folger's. If she had they might never have saved Sinbad from the cruel boys.

The New Pet

Next morning Lucretia and Thomas hurried downstairs as soon as they were dressed. They were eager to see how Sinbad had fared.

"But where is he?" Lucretia asked in dismay. The tern's basket was overturned. She could not see him anywhere.

"I didn't think he could get out of his basket," said Thomas. "He must have tried to fly. Look, there are marks everywhere."

"But where could he have gone?" Lucretia asked. "The house is closed up tight. The only way he could have gotten out is by flying up the chimney. Do you think he could do that?"

50

They looked about in dismay. Wood ashes and bird tracks streaked the floor. Sinbad must have fluttered around near the fireplace. Wood shavings, to light the fire, had been spilled out of the old earthenware crock on the hearth.

"Mercy!" thought Lucretia. "If Sinbad can do that, he might easily set the house afire. Suppose there had been live ashes on the hearth!" She and Thomas picked up the shavings hastily.

Peering under chairs and tables, Lucretia suddenly spied the tern. Sinbad was on the floor in a dark corner over by the kitchen dresser. Except for his trailing wing he looked quite spry. His bright, shoe-button eyes watched every move they made. He seemed to be saying, "It's about time you came down and fed me. I had to hunt around for myself. Get me something to eat, but don't you come too close!"

"Hello, Sinbad! Good Sinbad! We'll get thee something to eat."

51

Squatting on their heels, Lucretia and Thomas coaxed the bird gently. But he did not stir in his corner. His eyes stayed watchful. When Thomas put out his hand to touch him, Sinbad opened his beak. Thomas wisely drew back his hand.

"I'll dig some clams for thee as soon as school is out—see if I don't," he promised. "I know thee would like clams better than bread or mush. I'll get thee all thee can eat."

Lucretia and Thomas swept Mother's kitchen floor clean before they ate. They knew that if they wanted to keep Sinbad they must show her a spotless house when she came home.

"Get the breakfast mush, Lucretia. It's in the cold room by the molasses jug," Thomas ordered, when they had finished. "I'll build the fire."

He stuffed some shavings under a few sticks of wood. He struck a piece of flint against an old axhead which lay on the hearth and lighted the pile. It blazed up into a fine crackling glow.

Lucretia spooned some of the cold mush into an iron pot. She added some water from the dipper in the pail by the fireside. Then she hung the pot over the flames. It felt good to stand near a hot fire and stir porridge, Lucretia thought. She gave a small shiver.

The March wind was still shaking the windows as though it wanted to get into the house. Some of it did blow in. She could feel it even through her thick homespun dress. It took a long time for the heat from the great kitchen fireplace to creep upstairs. There was a damp morning chill in the big house.

The glow and comfort in the kitchen reached Sinbad in his corner. Lucretia and Thomas sat down to their bowls of mush. They could hear Sinbad pecking at the cold porridge. He wouldn't touch it while they were watching him. He watched them suspiciously and stopped eating as soon as they looked at him.

"I've been thinking how to fix a place for Sinbad," said Thomas. He watched Lucretia pour a rich, golden river of molasses over her mush. What a lot she was taking without Mother to check her!

"Here, greedy!" He grabbed the jug with the cool firmness of an older brother. He helped himself generously.

"Sinbad is a wild bird," Thomas went on. "He won't like to be shut up in a pen. That's why he chose that corner. I wish we could leave him there. What do you suppose Mother would say if we let him stay in that corner?"

"Mother says gulls and terns are as dirty as chickens," Lucretia reminded him.

"A big wooden box laid on its side would give him a corner," said Thomas.

"We'll put the box right by the back door. We can play with him there," agreed Lucretia, as though that were settled.

54

"But where will we get it? Who's going to give us a box?" Thomas demanded. "Thee knows that all the families on the island need many more boxes than they can get."

He was right. Who could spare them a box? On their island every bit of wood was precious. Like everything else, it came from the Continent. There was never too much of anything on Nantucket—except sand! Everything on the island had to be saved and used year after year.

"Maybe Mr. Coleman would spare a box from his candle factory if thee ran errands for him after school," Lucretia suggested.

Thomas shook his head. "I don't want to ask him. David and I aren't friends any more."

Lucretia was too astonished to speak for a minute. The Coleman family lived on Fair Street too. David was the same age as Thomas. The two boys liked to do the same things, and they always spent all their spare time together.

"We quarreled the other day," Thomas explained. "It was the day David's mother sent him to the big windmill on the commons with some corn. I went along. While we were waiting for the corn to be ground the miller sighted a ship. It was flying Starbuck's flag."

"I remember," said Lucretia. "Thee won the race home and got the silver dollar Cousin Eliza Starbuck gives for news of a Starbuck ship."

"Yes, and I spent it on a knife to carve the ring Obed is helping me with," Thomas added sadly. "I almost wish I hadn't. Then I could buy Sinbad a box. I should have saved the money instead of spending it so quickly without thinking. That's what Mother told me."

"But what made thee quarrel with David? He has always been thy best friend."

"He said I ought to divide the dollar with him, because I wouldn't have thought of going to the mill that day alone."

"Well, I never!" cried Lucretia. "There'll be lots of other chances for David. Right now Mother has a silver dollar on the mantel in our Great Room. It's waiting for the boy who brings her the first word that Father's boat has been sighted. He might get that."

"I know." Thomas nodded. "I told David he was acting like a baby. We haven't spoken to each other since."

Lucretia had eaten her way to the bottom of her porridge bowl. "Look," she said proudly, "I've eaten every bit."

"No wonder, with all that molasses. . . . Lucretia, I have it!" Thomas slapped his hand suddenly on his knee. "Maybe I can pump water for the Widow Mitchell. She gives boys a penny a bucket. I'll run and ask her before school."

"The fire—it hasn't been put out," Lucretia called after him as he dashed out of the kitchen. "Remember what Mother said!"

"Fiddlesticks! It's almost out now. Thee can fix it. And don't forget thy sixty rows of knitting!" The front door slammed.

Left alone, Lucretia stacked the porridge bowls and spoons neatly. Today she would have to wait until suppertime to wash them. She wasn't big enough to lift the heavy water kettle off the crane. She would need Thomas' help.

As for the fire, there were, as Thomas had said, only a few embers left. She poured water on them with the dipper. She had often seen Mother do that. Then Lucretia threw on a shovelful of sand from the sandbox on the hearth.

After that she got her knitting. It was her task and Sally's to knit all the family stockings. Lucretia sat on the floor beside Sinbad. If she knitted fast she knew she could do seventy-five rows before Mother got home tomorrow. Her knitting needles flashed briskly. This time she would surprise Mother.

"We're going to do all our chores the best we know how, Sinbad. Then maybe Mother won't mind thy staying," Lucretia told him. She could see that Sinbad was interested.

"I'm going to eat all my mush every day too. I started this morning. If thee eats mush every day thee'll get strong and well. Thy feathers won't look rumpled. They'll become sleek and smooth."

Lucretia paused to see if Sinbad took to the idea. He blinked one eye drowsily at her.

"He really understands," thought the little girl. She went on talking to him. "I have two sisters, one big and one small. I'll repeat their names for thee. It was important for a bird to know about the family he had come to live with.

By the time the school bell rang Sinbad was fast asleep. Lucretia had added several inches to her knitting. She put a bowl of water and some moist bread beside the sleeping tern. Then she ran upstairs and out of the house to school.

Fire!

THE NEW girl sat on the same school bench with Lucretia. Her name was Phoebe Worth. Her small, fat hand pressed her pencil down too hard on her slate. The pencil squeaked as she wrote across the slate. Because she was trying to do a sum, her round face wore a puzzled frown. Lucretia could see that Phoebe didn't know much about arithmetic.

The scratching of Phoebe's pencil made Lucretia wriggle uncomfortably. "Oh, dear!" thought Lucretia. "If Master Higgins notices he'll speak sharply to Phoebe. Then she'll get more muddled than ever."

She glanced at the little girl's slate. It was easy to see where Phoebe had made a mistake.

Lucretia wrote on the back of her own slate, "3 × 3 = 9." She showed it to Phoebe. Phoebe nodded quickly and rubbed out what she had done. She started all over again. But the anxious look did not leave her face.

"Brother!" Lucretia thought again. "I could do it for her in a jiffy, but that would be cheating. Poor Phoebe! Now Master Higgins will have to explain all over again and keep us in late. It makes the other girls impatient with her."

Lucretia's own work was finished. Her thoughts wandered to her sister. What a lot Sally would have to tell them about the new lambs! And Lucretia and Thomas would have Sinbad to show her. Lucretia imagined Sally's pleasure and surprise over Sinbad. It would be even more fun to see Betsy's face when she saw the tern. Betsy would enjoy a pet too.

Suddenly, far off and very faint, she heard the sound of a horn. It was coming closer. She sat still, listening. Yes, it must be Jerry, the town crier. Every girl in the room looked up from her slate. Master Higgins had been hearing a spelling class. He stopped in the middle of a word to listen. The room was very quiet.

Suddenly from outside came the noise of running feet. Then a shout. Lucretia heard windows thrown open. Women called to one another across the street.

The horn was drawing nearer and louder all the time. Now voice after voice took up the cry. "Fire! Fire! Fire!"

Right away Lucretia thought of Sinbad. He had upset the shavings last night. Suppose he had done it again! Suppose she had not put the fire out completely this morning! Why hadn't she or Thomas thought to put the shavings out on the back stoop before they left for school?

Lucretia hardly heard the babble of voices that rose as Master Higgins dismissed school. When there was a fire in Nantucket, every man, woman and child dropped everything and ran out to help. Lucretia remembered that if Mother had been home Sinbad would never have been allowed in the kitchen. Mother had left the house in their care. Had it been set afire through their carelessness? She crowded down the stairs with the other pupils. The talk of the older girls made her realize how serious a fire could be.

"There's a strong wind today," said one.

"Yes, lucky it's still from the northeast. The fire's not likely to get to the harbor."

"Unless the wind changes," young Anna Starbuck reminded them. "If the barrels of whale oil that are stacked on the wharves should catch, my father says it would make a blaze no one could put out. That's why fires are so dangerous on Nantucket."

"Let's hurry. We're old enough to pass buckets now!" said one of the older girls.

The girls of the Quaker school on Nabby Bailey's Lane poured through the door. They were pushing, laughing with excitement, happy to be let out. Phoebe Worth clung to Lucretia's arm.

"Where's the fire?" everyone kept asking.

Lucretia held her breath. It was a question she did not dare ask.

"On Plum Lane," someone answered.

Lucretia's heart gave a thankful bound. Plum Lane was not Fair Street. It was not far away, and she was sorry of course for the people whose house was burning. But at least she and Thomas were not to blame. Thomas' school was on Pleasant Street. She wondered if it had been let out. He must be anxious too.

Just then Caleb Macy pushed his way through the crowd of girls on his way to help put out the fire. He went to school with Thomas.

"Thy brother's already gone home, Lucretia," he called to her. "The fire is pretty close to thy house."

"I'm going home too, Phoebe," Lucretia said to the little girl.

"Please let me stay with thee," pleaded Phoebe. "There won't be anyone at my house. Great-aunt Dorcas went to 'Sconset."

Phoebe was an orphan from Cape Cod, Lucretia remembered. She had come to Nantucket only a few months ago to live with her aunt. As yet she had no playmates.

"Come on then." Lucretia started to run. "But we have to hurry."

Already smoke was rising in a great cloud above Plum Lane. Townspeople passed them, all on the run. Women had hastily thrown shawls over their heads. They all carried buckets they had snatched from their stoops. Everyone was supposed to bring at least two.

Ahead, Lucretia could see men hauling the newest fire-fighting machine. It was a hand pump on wheels. It had a leather hose.

A long line of women and girls had formed at the corner of Martin's Lane and Fair Street. That was where the village pump stood. Thomas was there with the older boys. As soon as the boys pumped a bucket of water it was passed from hand to hand until it reached the men who were trying to put out the fire on Plum Lane.

Lucretia rushed on. She could see smoke blowing toward home. She must get back to Sinbad! Her breath seemed stuck in her throat. Behind her she heard Phoebe panting.

Now at last she had reached her own street. The Widow Mitchell was running from house to house. She pounded door knockers to warn people. She always imagined others were as hard of hearing as she was. Most of the people were already trying to put out the fire.

"Thee is just in time," she shouted to Lucretia. "Right now Thomas is needed at the pump. Thee'll have to go up on thy walk." She pointed to the lookout on top of the Coffin house. "The wind's blowing this way. It's Nathan Brown's woodpile that's burning. He let it get a head start. Just like his carelessness! Watch out for sparks on the roof. I'll go in with thee to unfasten the trap door.

"I might know this would happen while thy mother's gone." The Widow Mitchell went on scolding as they entered the house. "If people must go trading on the Continent, it's their own fault if something happens while they're away. Where does Anna keep her brooms?" She started down the kitchen stairs.

"Wait here, Phoebe." Lucretia left her breathless little friend in the front hall and hurried downstairs after the widow. She could never explain about Sinbad to Mrs. Mitchell.

Lucretia hoped to goodness Sinbad had stayed out of sight in his corner. But he hadn't, of course! He was squatting in the middle of the floor with every feather ruffled. It was plain he had no more love for the Widow Mitchell than she had for him.

"Mercy on us!" Mrs. Mitchell was exclaiming. "How did this creature get into the house, Lucretia?"

"We found him by the harbor." Lucretia put her mouth close to Mrs. Mitchell's ear. "He's hurt. We're going to take care of him."

"Don't shout so, child. I hear perfectly," Mrs. Mitchell replied. "Look there!" She pointed in disgust at the fresh tracks Sinbad had made on the floor. "Thy mother will have plenty to say about that, I expect," she added tartly. "There's no time to do anything about him now," she decided. Lucretia sighed in relief.

They took the brooms upstairs to the attic. There for the first time Mrs. Mitchell noticed Phoebe. "Who's this?" she asked. When Lucretia told her, she remarked loudly, just as though Phoebe couldn't hear, "Thought she didn't look like any of thy family. The Coffins and the Folgers don't run to fat."

69

She unfastened the trap door at the top of the attic ladder. "Now listen carefully, children," Mrs. Mitchell told them. "On a windy day almost anything can happen to a fire. If it jumps to this side of the street, Lucretia, thee must spread wet blankets on the roof."

She raised the trap door. The three of them stepped out onto the wooden platform or walk built over the peak of the roof. The platform looked like an open porch. Lucretia had never been allowed up here without Mother. Even now, with the danger of fire, she liked the feeling the walk gave her. It was like standing on top of the world. She could see over the whole town to the ocean.

"Just as I thought!" exclaimed Mrs. Mitchell. "Hot ashes are beginning to drop here. Stamp them out with your feet, children. Sparks may land on the slant of the roof, Lucretia. Then use the long-handled broom to beat them out."

The girls began to stamp on the sparks. Now and then they had to beat out sparks with the broom. They watched other children stamping on sparks on other roofs.

"As soon as we get more people to pump, Thomas can come up and help you," Mrs. Mitchell went on. "My own house needs watching, so I can't stay."

Lucretia didn't know whether to be glad or sorry when the Widow Mitchell's head disappeared down the ladder. Suppose Thomas was a long time coming? Suppose sparks fell on a part of the roof she and Phoebe couldn't reach!

Good Neighbors

PLUMP LITTLE Phoebe had never been on a roof-
top before. At first she felt dizzy. She had to
cling to the railing. Then she saw boys and girls
on the walks of other houses on Fair Street. Like
herself and Lucretia, they had been sent up to
put out sparks that might fall. "If they're not
afraid, I'm not going to be," Phoebe decided.
As she got busy stamping and using her broom
on the hot cinders she forgot about her fear.

There were moments when the wind shifted a
little. Then the smoke and sparks drifted in another direction and did not fall on Lucretia's
house, and the girls had a short rest.

72

They could look about them at the people below. Someone in the bucket brigade had started a sea chantey. This one was a song sailors sang when they hauled up the anchor. The crowd took up the rhythm as they passed the water buckets from hand to hand.

Lucretia felt her spine tingle. Men and women singing together. What a beautiful sound it made. She was a Quaker child, and Quakers believed it was wrong to sing. As she listened Lucretia began to wonder about that. Surely when trouble threatened it was a brave thing for people to raise their voices in song.

A great gust of wind blew cinders and ashes over the walk again. For a few minutes Lucretia and Phoebe forgot everything but the need to put them out. Then the wind died down and another pause came. The girls saw that the fire had done just what the Widow Mitchell had feared. It had jumped to their side of the street!

The barn next door had caught fire. It must have been burning for some time before anyone noticed it. Flames were already licking a corner of the roof.

"Get the horses and cow out of the barn!" Lucretia heard someone shout. But just then the burning woodpile on Nathan Brown's place collapsed. Cries for help came from that direction too. Flames taller than a house leaped up from the woodpile. Sparks shot high into the air. They drifted toward Lucretia and Phoebe and began to drop on the walk and roof.

Real fire was raining down on them suddenly. Lucretia forgot all about the barn. She could fight only one danger at a time. She and Phoebe had to work fast, stamping and beating. Some of the sparks fell on their dresses and burned small holes in the cloth. The girls brushed off these sparks and kept working. Fresh sparks continued to blow on the roof.

Finally the wind dropped again for a while. As they stood leaning on their brooms, resting, a great cheer rose from below. The girls peered over the railing to see.

"Someone has rescued the animals from the barn. Look, Lucretia," cried Phoebe. "They got them out just in time."

Phoebe was right—it was just in time. Red flames pierced the smoke coming from the barn. Their glare lighted the faces of two boys who were leading out a pair of struggling horses.

"Why, it's Thomas and David who did it! Hurrah!" yelled Lucretia. She waved her broom in excitement. Almost immediately, however, the frightened creatures broke away from the boys. They charged down the street and disappeared.

The next instant Lucretia and Phoebe were startled by a crash! The roof of the barn had fallen in!

"Watch out, Phoebe!" cried Lucretia.

The air was filled now with flaming bits of wood. No amount of stamping would put these out. The two little girls beat them desperately with their brooms.

"Blankets—spread wet blankets on the roof if the fire jumps to this side." That was what the Widow Mitchell had said before she left.

"But it's too late! We haven't time to go down and get blankets," Lucretia told herself frantically. "We should have brought them up when we came."

The smoke made Lucretia's eyes water. She could hardly see. Phoebe's round face too was smudged from the tears rolling down it. But she hadn't once said she was afraid—not even when the wind blew such a hot, choking blast that they had to turn their backs to it.

Sparks were landing now where Lucretia's short arms could not reach them. Even the long-handled broom would not reach.

If only Thomas would come! The crackle of the flames and the shouts of the people fighting the barn fire sounded very close. Stinging red cinders fell on the children. Here was a new danger! They had to drop their brooms and brush the cinders off each other's clothes and hair with their hands. These cinders were much larger, and they fell much more frequently.

Then suddenly through the confusion and noise, Lucretia heard her name called. She turned to find Thomas beside her! She thought she had never been so glad to see anyone!

"Go down into the house," he was shouting. "Get as many blankets as thee can, thee and Phoebe. Please hurry! And give us these——"

He snatched the broom she had just dropped. There was big Ben Coleman taking Phoebe's from her. Help had come at last! Everything was going to be all right now! All of a sudden Lucretia wanted to cry, but there wasn't time.

How she and Phoebe climbed down the attic ladder on their shaky legs she never knew. But somehow they did. They ran from room to room. They tore the blankets off every bed, rushed back to the attic with them. They handed them up through the trap door to Thomas and Ben. On the stairs they bumped into David Coleman. He was carrying water up to the roof to wet the blankets. The house was suddenly alive with boys and girls, and all of them were working.

Jonathan, Sam, Caleb and Will trooped in with more buckets of water. Other boys were setting ladders up against the front and back of the house. Hannah, Debbie and Lydia had brought extra brooms. The boys on the ladders helped Thomas and Ben, upon the walk, spread wet blankets over both sides of the roof.

Lucretia and Phoebe worked outside now with the older girls. All of them worked to put out the sparks that fell in the yard.

Meanwhile the alarm of the new fire had spread. Men came running from the wharves. Many expert hands were now at work. In a short while Nathan Brown's woodpile was a heap of wet ashes. Finally the barn fire was under control and no longer a danger. Two hours later the last ember was put out. A cheer rose from the women and girls. They had been steadily passing buckets all this time.

As usual after a fire in Nantucket, everyone was very thankful there had been no change in the wind. The ships and the hundreds of barrels of whale oil stacked on the wharves were safe. It was an occasion to celebrate!

The whaling crews went back to their ships singing and joking noisily. Silver coins jingled in their pockets. They had been well paid for their help. Neighbors opened their doors to one another. Everyone wanted to discuss the day's excitement over a dish of tea.

Thomas and Lucretia wanted to show Sinbad off to their friends. Luckily Mother had left a crock full of molasses cookies in the cold room. So, after the blankets had been taken down and hung in the yard to dry, they had a party in the Coffin kitchen.

But the excitement in the house—so many people calling to one another and running up and downstairs—had been too much for Sinbad. It took a long while to find him. He had managed to get underneath the kitchen dresser. It was dark and quiet there and he felt safe.

"He'll come out fast enough by himself," said Jonathan, "if we put some food near by and leave him alone."

"I had a tame crow once," Caleb told them. "I'll wager thee can teach this tern to come when thee whistles, same as I did the crow."

Hannah, Debbie, Lydia and Phoebe helped Lucretia tidy up the kitchen floor.

81

"We don't know where to keep Sinbad," said Lucretia. "Mother won't want him in the house."

"I've an idea!" David exclaimed. "Elder Prichard said he'd give Thomas and me each a dollar for saving his horse and cow. Say, Thomas, let's buy some wood and build Sinbad a fine house. I know just how to make it."

"There's no time to lose!" Thomas started gaily for the door.

"We'll help," Caleb offered.

"Beat you to the lumberyard,'" Jonathan shouted. "I can beat you any time!"

The boys were off. The racket they made faded. The kitchen now seemed peaceful.

Phoebe looked around wistfully. "I guess I ought to go home now. Aunt Dorcas will be wondering where I am."

"Let's go with her," Lydia suggested. "Aunt Dorcas ought to hear how Phoebe proved herself a real Nantucketer today."

"She's an Islander now," agreed Hannah. "We'll take her to pick cranberries in the bogs next. She'll like that."

"And sheepshearing!" exclaimed Lucretia, clapping her hands. "Thee hasn't been to a sheepshearing yet, Phoebe. My father will take us. His ship is due back any day now."

The girls all went together to Trader's Lane where Phoebe lived. The little fat girl dashed into her house ahead of the others.

"Aunt Dorcas! Listen, Aunt Dorcas! I'm not an off-islander any more, I'm an Islander! They said so." She shouted the good news.

"Aye, there's nothing like sharing something together, even if it's trouble." Aunt Dorcas nodded wisely when she heard about Phoebe's part in fighting the fire. "Thee'll never be home-sick again, Phoebe, now thee is beginning to learn Nantucket ways. Thee'll find there is no other place like our island."

Grandfather Folger's calash was in front of the stoop when Lucretia got home again. He was talking to the Widow Mitchell and a neighbor. The two women had taken all the Coffin blankets off the line to wash them.

"By the time Anna comes home tomorrow, they'll be as fresh and clean as when she left," Mrs. Mitchell promised.

"She'll thank you both kindly for that, I know, ma'am," said Captain Folger. He smiled at Lucretia. "Well, mate, I hear thee took command of the ship till Thomas arrived. Better come home with me now and see those lambs."

How she wanted to go! But there was Sinbad. Lucretia explained about him to Grandfather. And what would Thomas think?

But Thomas arrived just then with David and an armful of lumber. He grinned his approval of the plan. In fact, she suspected that he was glad to have her go.

"David will stay with me. We'll finish Sinbad's box twice as fast with no one around to
ask questions. So hop along," he said good-
naturedly. He boosted Lucretia over the carriage wheel.

Lucretia turned to wave good-by from the
calash. She saw how glad the two boys were to
be left alone. The fire had made them friends
again. She thought of what Aunt Dorcas had
said: "There's nothing like sharing something
together, even if it's trouble."

Even the Widow Mitchell, with her blunt
manner and sharp tongue, was showing that she
was a good neighbor. The fire had taught Lucretia as well as Phoebe something about Nantucket ways. She would never forget them.

Father's Ship

SEVERAL WEEKS later, in the month of May, Sally and Lucretia were walking home from school. They went up the narrow, sandy lane that led to Fair Street.

"Mother's in. I can see the shutter of the shop window," Lucretia said.

When Mother opened the shutters of her shop, one of them stuck out beyond the corner of the house. To the children it was a signal that she was home. It always made the children happy.

"Goody!" cried Sally. "Let's see who gets there first!" Sally's longer legs covered ground easily, but Lucretia was lighter and quicker.

The two little girls reached the front door together. They were panting and laughing.

"I have good news," Mother called from inside the shop. Her voice had such a glad ring they knew right away what had happened.

"Father's home!" they shouted together.

"Yes, the 'Trial' dropped anchor in Woods Hole on Cape Cod yesterday. Captain Bunker brought the news by packet boat this morning."

Betsy banged a string of spools on the floor at Mother's feet. She didn't know what had happened, but she knew everybody was happy. She added her small racket to the general joy.

"But how did we miss seeing the 'Trial' sail past Nantucket?" Lucretia asked. "David Coleman has been watching every day. He hoped he could win that silver dollar on our mantel."

"Because wind and tide favored her sailing through Vineyard Sound instead. She made better time that way," Mother explained.

"That means we won't even see the 'Trial' this time." Sally made a long face. "I wish Father docked in Nantucket Harbor. It would be so much more fun. Most Nantucket children can go on board their fathers' boats."

"The 'Trial' has a deeper keel than the whaling ships. She can't sail over the Nantucket Bar. Thee knows that without being told, child."

"Will Father come tonight?" Lucretia's black eyes sparkled with eagerness.

"Tomorrow noon, Captain Bunker said. I sent Thomas to Grandfather Folger's with the news. Grandfather has been fattening one of his calves since Christmas for Father's return."

"A veal feast! We're going to celebrate with a veal feast!" Sally whirled joyfully on her toes. Her disappointment was forgotten.

"We'll have to cook all day tomorrow to welcome our sailor," Mother said. "You three must stay home from school to help."

"Here's Thomas! No school for thee tomorrow—did thee hear?" Lucretia rushed to her brother. He came leaping up the stoop.

"Knew it before thee," Thomas boasted. He was bursting with excitement.

"Mother," he asked, "if Obed is willing, may I sail out with him in his dory early tomorrow? Then I could meet Father and the Woods Hole packet. Father would really be surprised to see me there."

Mother shook her head. "Obed would lose part of his day's catch. And Captain Bunker would be to the trouble of coming about into the wind to take thee aboard 'Tis asking a great deal of both of them. Besides, I shall need thee here to keep a peat fire going. I shall heat both ovens tomorrow, and they'll need to be kept hot."

"Bother the cooking!" Thomas' face fell.

"I notice thee doesn't say so when thy share of food is set before thee." Mother laughed.

"If thee works here tomorrow, Sinbad won't fly off as soon as he's eaten the breakfast scraps we give him," Lucretia reminded Thomas.

"As long as he hears thy whistle he stays around," added Mother. "I should think thee would like to have Sinbad here to show Father."

"There'll be two surprises for him—Betsy and Sinbad." Lucretia clapped her hands delight.-edly. "We have a real welcome for him."

"Why, that's so." Sally hadn't thought of it until now. "Father has never seen Betsy, and she's more than two years old."

"Many Nantucket children are born while their fathers are away at sea," Mother told them. "I myself was twice as big as Betsy before I saw my father for the first time."

"What a pity Betsy is shy with strangers! It will spoil everything if she cries," Lucretia worried. "Father will be disappointed if she is afraid of him."

90

But Mother laughed at the idea. "Your father has a way with children. Thee will see. Now I have plenty of work for the three of you this afternoon. Thomas, after thee has laid a fire in the Great Room, I want all the candlesticks rubbed bright. The small coffeepot lamp that hangs from the chimney and the one by the door must be filled with sperm oil."

"Sally," Mother went on, "I've made some scouring paste from wood ashes. Thee can polish the pewter and silver. By the time thee has finished the scouring, the bread will be ready to knead. We must plan very carefully if we are to get all the baking done. As for thee, Lucretia, run to thy Cousin Macy's, then to thy Uncle William Coffin's, and last to thy Aunt Abigail's. Tell them the news, and also that we shall expect them here tomorrow evening at six. Yes, thee may say there is to be a veal feast if thee wishes to."

The packet from Woods Hole rounded Brant's Point and entered Nantucket Harbor. Sailors began to loosen the ropes to spill the wind out of her sails. She drifted down harbor to the wharf where she was to tie up.

A tall figure stood on her starboard deck waving a stovepipe hat. That must be Father, Lucretia decided. She swallowed hard. Excitement suddenly choked her. Sally and Thomas were dancing and shouting like a pair of Indians. Mother was holding Betsy high with both hands for Father to see. She didn't even seem to know tears were running down her face.

When Father had last sailed away, Lucretia had been only five. She could remember sitting on his lap. She could remember his gentle strength and the hearty ring of his voice. But she had almost forgotten his face. All at once she felt shy. When the gangplank was put down Sally and Thomas raced for it.

92

Lucretia did not follow them. She stayed be-hind with Mother and Betsy.

Townsfolk crowded to the dock's edge.

"Howdy, Cap'n Coffin!"

"What sort of passage round the Horn, Tom?"

She heard them greet Father, and stood on tip-toe to see him, but there were too many people.

Then the crowd parted. A broad-shouldered man with a bronzed face pushed eagerly through. "Anna!" he called, and Mother and Betsy were swept into a mighty hug.

The next thing she knew, Lucretia was swung high off her feet and soundly kissed. Father had come back into their lives like a rushing wind!

What a proud procession the family made, walking home to Fair Street! They were stopped every few yards. Everyone wanted to shake Fa-ther's hand. Betsy rode on his shoulder. She was crowing and laughing. She had made friends with him right away.

Thomas followed Father and Mother. He carried the "Trial's" compass. Sally had been given the roll of charts Father used to map his way across the ocean. Lucretia held his telescope carefully in both hands. Behind the children walked Jethro, Father's cabin boy, and a sailor from the packet. They lugged Captain Coffin's heavy sea chest between them. Lashed to the chest was a long, flat package.

"What's in it?" Thomas and Sally and Lucretia kept teasing Father to tell them.

"A dragon," Captain Coffin said gravely. He did not even wink at Mother. They could hardly wait to see. Lucretia wondered if Sinbad would like to have a dragon about.

Father did not say a word when he stepped inside his house. He stood still, looking at the shining order of the rooms. They were all glad, then, that they had worked hard to make the house welcome him.

Then they led him out to the yard to meet Sinbad. Father cupped his hands over his mouth and called just like a tern. Sinbad cocked his head and listened and came closer. Soon he was eating from Father's hand.

After that Father opened his sea chest.

"Mercy, Thomas! Thee must have paid a vast sum for it," scolded Mother when Father hung a fine Cashmere shawl over her shoulders. "It is too grand for a Quaker. I dare not wear it to Meeting!" But she stroked its soft, dark folds lovingly just the same.

Next Father pulled out a doll for Betsy. It had been made by the Carib Indians out of dried grass. The little girl hugged the doll. Then she hugged her father.

"Lucretia loves a gathering of friends—or she did before I went away," said Captain Coffin. He handed her a bulky parcel. Inside was a small blue and white teaset from China.

"Thee can hold make-believe conversations over a dish of tea, just like thy elders." He chuckled as she hugged him.

Sally's present was a box full of beautifully carved ivory jackstraws.

Then, while they all held their breath, Father undid the mysterious flat package. It was for Thomas—and what a present it was! A huge Chinese kite! On it was painted a fierce dragon. It had a real tail.

Later that afternoon all the relatives came to supper. The feast began with hot plum broth. Then came a great shoulder of roast veal, mashed potatoes whipped in cream, and golden baked squash. There were muffins called Indian puffs. Last came cold huckleberry pudding, with hard sauce made from Mother's best rose-flavored butter. All morning the good odor of roasting meat, fresh muffins and hot raisins stewing in sugar and nutmeg had teased the children.

They had been growing hungrier and hungrier. Now there was plenty for everybody—even enough for Thomas and the other boys.

People in Nantucket always held an evening's "conversation" when a seafarer came home. After supper neighbors dropped in. Sally opened the front door for the guests. Lucretia led them to the Great Room. There chairs had been drawn up in front of a cheerful fire.

"Do come and join the circle," Lucretia said. She showed each guest politely to a chair, as Mother had taught her.

Soon the Great Room buzzed with talk. Sally and Thomas played quietly in a corner with the new jackstraws. But Lucretia wanted to sit close to Father and listen. She wanted to hear about the places where Father had been.

Father asked many questions. Two years ago, when he had gone away, there had been talk of war between France and America.

98

"We Yankees may not have a Navy, but our privateers have taught French ships to stay on their side of the Atlantic." Mr. Will Gardner rubbed his hands with satisfaction.

"Aye, it is a pity President Adams accepted the French peace offer. We might have given them a good licking," said Captain Hussey.

"John Adams did well to make peace." Grandfather stuck to his Quaker ideas firmly. "Quarrels are only made worse by going to war. I wish there were more of the world's leaders like him."

After that talk drifted to General George Washington, the nation's first President. He had died six months ago. Father was sorry to hear this news. Everyone agreed Washington had been a great soldier and an honest statesman.

Lucretia was listening so hard she did not notice how dark it was getting. At last Mother took a long wood-shaving from the wood basket, held it to the fire and told her to light the candles.

It was Father's turn now to tell the company all about his voyage. This was what Lucretia had been waiting to hear. Thomas was sent to the cellar for fresh logs and a jug of cider.

The clock struck ten. Lucretia hoped Mother hadn't heard it, but Anna Coffin looked up. Her eyes traveled to Lucretia's flushed face. They caught Sally in the middle of a yawn.

"It is high time little girls were in bed," she said firmly. Sally and Lucretia went obediently.

Lucretia lay awake a long time, thinking about what she had heard. She wanted to learn a great deal. She wanted to grow up to be a patriot. It would be nice to be a statesman, too, maybe a President. It was queer that no one had mentioned the name of a woman President tonight.

"I will ask Father why," Lucretia said to herself just before she fell asleep.

The Shearing
Grounds

ON THE second Monday in June, Mother, Sally and Lucretia were up at dawn. They began at once to pack several big hampers of food. These they were going to take to the shearing grounds by the shores of Miacomet Pond. Father and Thomas were out in the yard harnessing Toby, the brown pony, and Molly, the black mare, to two tip-carts. They would all ride to the south side of the island.

"One, two, three, four, five—my, what a lot of chicken pies!" said Sally. "Won't they taste good out at the shearing grounds." She set the last one down by the meat hamper.

101

"Now go back to the pantry," Mother told her. "Bring the brown crock full of rose butter and the blue crock full of pot cheese. Lucretia thee will find three dozen plum tarts on a tray on the lower shelf. Be careful not to spill them."

"There, I've wrapped the poundcake, the ginger loaves, the white loaves and the corn muffins all in clean napkins." Phoebe Worth counted the items off on her fingers. She had been invited to spend the days at the shearing grounds with the Coffin family. "Shall I pack them in the bread hamper now, Mrs. Coffin?"

"Yes, Phoebe. And there are four Indian puddings, a platter of cranberry dumplings and a pail of huckleberries still to be brought from the pantry. Sally can help thee."

"My, such a lot of food!" thought Phoebe.

"No wonder thee and Sally have spent this last week helping your mother cook! It's enough to feed an army!" she exclaimed out loud.

"But not too much," Sally said. "We shall spend two whole days on the shearing grounds, thee knows. Besides, visitors from the mainland come, and we share our food with strangers as well as friends. Everyone works hard and gets awfully hungry!"

At last everything was packed and they were ready to start.

Father placed a kitchen chair for Mother in the cart he would drive. When she was seated, the hampers of food, the pewter plates and mugs, the linen and tableware and blankets were stowed in. Then Betsy was lifted onto Mother's lap. A hook held the forward part of the tip-cart down. Otherwise the weight of the people in it would have tipped the cart and spilled out the people and the hampers.

Father climbed in. He had just enough room to stand beside Mother's chair. He gathered up Molly's reins and turned to Thomas.

"Remember, don't loiter, lad! Follow as soon as possible with thy sisters. The two of us must set up the tent for Mother before we help with the herding."

"Yes, sir." Thomas grinned happily. It was the first time he had been trusted to drive a cart by himself. He was feeling pretty important.

As soon as Father and Mother left, Thomas began to load his own cart. "Help me hoist all this canvas in," he ordered Sally, Lucretia and Phoebe. He picked up an armful of worn and weathered sails. He and Father had brought a pile of them down from the attic.

"Step lively now, mates," he sang out. They had lifted in the last bundle. "Hop in and hold fast to the rope across the cart. We shall steer a rough course over the commons!"

" 'Tis a real lark!" The three little girls laughed and settled themselves on the floor of the cart. They dangled their feet out the back.

104

"Giddap!" Thomas said to the pony.

Toby had been pawing the sandy road. He was impatient to follow the mare. He started so suddenly now that Sally and Lucretia and Phoebe were thrown forward. They all giggled as they clutched the rope.

Then before they could right themselves, the cart went bump—bump—bump—across the cobblestones on Main Street. It turned up Center Street, heading for the commons. Thomas drove standing up, with his feet braced against the sides of the cart. How he wished David Coleman could see him now. He didn't think David could drive as fast as this! The pony heard the gales of laughter behind him. He pricked up his ears and broke into a gallop.

The tip-cart swayed from side to side. Lucretia's cotton sunbonnet hung under her chin. Sally had lost hers among the sails. Phoebe's nearly flew out of the cart.

Sally noticed the stern looks that followed their rollicking passage through the streets. Other Nantucket families were on their way to the shearing grounds, but they were traveling quietly. Sally know what the neighbors must think about the cloud of dust Thomas raised and the racket they all made. It would be sure to reach Mother's ears that the Coffin children had broken the Quaker rules of behavior.

"Stop, Thomas! Stop go-ing so fa-ast!" The words were jolted out of Sally, for just then they reached the commons.

It was certainly bumpy going over the moors where there were no roads. Toby the pony wanted to go slow, but Thomas urged him on.

He grinned back at his jostled passengers. "Father said to hurry."

"Wa-ait till we reach Mia-co-met Pond," Lucretia told Sally and Phoebe between bounces. "We'll pa-pay him back then!"

106

Up and down the hummocks they jounced. The scent of crushed sweet fern and bay leaf rose under the cart wheels. The sun climbed higher in the sky. The bare, unshaded moors were hot under its glare. But as they neared the south shore of the island, the wind blew fresh from the sea. They breathed deeply.

"There's Miacomet Pond." Sally showed Phoebe a long, narrow strip of water ahead of them. "It's—it's a mile long," she added. She had to grab suddenly at the rope as the cart swung sharply around a clump of bushes. "It ends right at the ocean beach."

Already they were passing rows of sheeppens which lined the shores of the pond. "Each family has its own pens for shearing and its own washing place," Thomas told Phoebe. "We always have fun here." As they topped a rise of ground he cried, "There are Father and Mother and Betsy waiting for us."

"Quick, get ready to jump out of the cart!" Lucretia poked Sally and Phoebe. "This is the time to play our trick on Thomas."

They waited until a tangle of huckleberry bushes slowed the cart. Here was their chance. They slid quietly to the ground. Thomas, who was intent on cutting a fine figure before Father, did not turn his head.

"Hang on! Here we go!" he shouted. He slapped the reins over Toby's back. The pony broke into a gallop again and the cart, with so much weight gone, fairly flew.

Sally laughed. "He's planning to dump us."

"Wait and see how surprised he'll be!" cried Lucretia gleefully.

The girls followed on foot. Thomas, they could see, was stooping over. He meant to unfasten the hook which held the tip-cart straight. But the pony caught sight of the mare grazing a little distance away.

108

Just as Thomas undid the hook the pony turned in the direction of the mare. Thomas was thrown off balance. Up tipped the cart and out he went, his heels sawing the air. Father and Mother laughed as hard as the girls.

Father gave Thomas a long look as he scrambled to his feet. His face was very red. "I have no doubt," Father said, "that thee planned it otherwise. Thy sisters were too smart for thee."

Before they went to herd the sheep, Father and Thomas made a comfortable shelter for Mother and Betsy and the hampers of food. They stretched old sails over poles. All along the shores of the pond other people were busy doing the same thing. All the children enjoyed sheep shearing time and wished it lasted longer.

"You can take Betsy for a walk now, but don't go far," Mother told the three girls that afternoon. They had all eaten lunch. The supplies had been stacked tidily in the shelter.

Lucretia and Sally were eager to show Phoebe all the Nantucket customs. They strolled along the edge of the high, sandy bluffs. Below lay the beach and the ocean. The roar of the surf was a new sound to Phoebe.

On their left the shearing grounds were dotted with tents and groups of busy people.

"See the men hammering on that big wooden platform! That's for the dancing tomorrow, after the sheep are sheared," said Lucretia.

"Dancing! Are you allowed to dance?" asked Phoebe, astonished.

"Oh, it's not for us Quakers," Sally explained, "but we can watch."

"Here come the flying horses from the Continent!" cried Lucretia excitedly. She pointed to the brightly painted merry-go-round that was being drawn across the fields.

"And there are the gypsy fortune-tellers," Sally added. They were coming to a group of dark-skinned men and women near a shelter by a fire. The women wore scarlet kerchiefs on their heads. Their skirts were every color Phoebe could think of. The golden rings in their ears tinkled when they walked. They looked shabby.

"Mother says to keep away from them," Lucretia reminded the girls. She steered Betsy in another direction. "Sometimes they steal things out of our tents.

"Look," she cried suddenly, "the sheep are coming! I see hundreds of them! Help me hold Betsy up so she may see."

"Why, they look like moving water," Phoebe marveled. Waves of closely massed sheep rippled over the top of the ridge. They flowed downward to the shores of Miacomet Pond.

Sally and Lucretia made a chair of their hands for Betsy. Now they could all get back quickly to tell Mother. From their own tent they had a fine view of the oncoming herd. Behind the running sheep, boys and men in tip-carts drove the animals. On either side of the carts more herders advanced on foot, holding hands. They hemmed in the sheep that strayed or ran blindly out of the herd in their fright.

"I see Thomas!" Lucretia was the first to recognize him.

"And Father—in the other cart alongside him," added Mother.

Soon the shores of the pond swarmed with animals. The air was full of the frantic baaing of ewes calling their lambs. The men tried to separate their flocks from the main herd. At last each owner was satisfied he had driven his own sheep into the sheeppen reserved for him.

Then, one by one all the animals were plunged into the pond. The brambles that clung to their wool had to be washed out. The animals, frightened, fought and kicked.

Lucretia saw Thomas and Father, knee-deep in the water. They were struggling with a stubborn ram. It would not stand still to be scrubbed. She longed to be nearer the fun. As though she understood, Mother took Betsy from her and nodded to the three children.

"All right, girls, you may run down to the bank so that Phoebe may see it all. Only don't get in anyone's way. Tempers are short at shearingtime! Everyone has to work fast."

"The darling lambs!" cried Phoebe, leaning over a pen to rub a small wooly head.

"This one will grow horns and be a ram." Lucretia showed her two hard lumps on its forehead. "I hope he'll be better tempered than Samson." She pointed to the big ram whose head was held tight between Thomas' knees. Father was washing him with a stiff brush.

Father gave the animal a final rub. "Let him go," he sang out to Thomas. Samson did not wait a second. With a violent push he knocked Thomas over. Then he charged up the narrow runway from the pond to the pen.

Thomas sat down with a splash in the shallow water. It was the second time he had come to grief that day—and before a lot of people too!

114

"It's all in the day's work, lad." Father laughed and gave him a hand up. Thomas might have laughed too if he hadn't seen Lucretia and Sally and Phoebe watching and giggling.

He frowned at his sisters as he followed Samson into the pen to shoo another sheep into the pond. "Why aren't you helping Mother?" he asked. "You just get in our way!"

"She said we could come and watch. So there!" Sally answered tartly.

"Besides, we're helping here, too," Lucretia said. She picked up a stick one of the herders had dropped. Running to the sheep which had stopped midway to the pond, she gave it a poke through the fencing around the runway. With a frightened *"Baa-aa!"* it ran straight into the pond and stood still.

"See!" cried Lucretia, very pleased with herself. "Thee and Father can do the washing, and we'll drive the lambs down. It will save time."

"Oh, will it?" Thomas turned on her. "Well, the sheep are none of thy business, Lucretia Coffin! Go back to the tents with the women and girls where thee belongs. This is men's work! We don't need thee here!"

"Thee is being horrid because thee got dumped out of the cart instead of us. I can't abide thee!" blazed Lucretia.

"Sally! Lucretia! Phoebe!" To Thomas' great satisfaction, Mother's call came soaring over their angry voices. It was time for supper.

The girls ran back to the shelter. Mrs. Coffin had already put out the food.

"You children must eat now. The shearers will soon start coming from the pond to be fed," said Mother. "Betsy, thank goodness, is sound asleep in that corner. She'll not stir until morning. We shall have our hands full serving hungry crews of men and boys. I will need thee to help me as soon as they come."

116

By evening Sally, Lucretia and Phoebe were tired out with fun and excitement. All day long they had been out in the sun and wind. It made them drowsy. They were glad to curl up under the blankets beside Betsy. The soothing *swish-swash* of the ocean waves sounded all during the night and flowed through their dreams.

Lucretia's Punishment

NEXT MORNING they could not go to the pond at all. Mother had a hundred things for them to do. Sally must run to the spring for still another bucket of water. Phoebe must carry six tarts and an extra chicken pie to Grandmother Folger's tent. Lucretia, who never got messages muddled, went from one tent to another on errands for Mother. In between times the girls took turns minding Betsy.

Finally, in the middle of the afternoon, Mother gave them leave to watch the shearing. The three little girls hurried back to the pond. Thomas and Father were still at work.

Phoebe was surprised to find the ground of the shearing pen covered with old sails.

"Father spreads them on the ground before the sheep are clipped," Lucretia told her.

"It keeps the wool clean. And it makes it easier to gather up and carry home in the carts," explained Sally. "If the wool wasn't wrapped up, loose pieces would blow all over the moors."

"Plenty of it gets lost that way," remarked Thomas. He seemed to have forgotten his crossness yesterday. "Look!" He pointed across the pond. "See the wool floating in the air."

Phoebe looked. She had not noticed before the wisps of grayish wool drifting back toward the village of Nantucket—here a piece and there a piece, but enough to be useful.

"It's an ill wind that blows nobody good," Father quoted. "By the end of the day, Phoebe, thee will see a great many townsfolk on the edge of the shearing grounds."

119

"What will they do there?" asked Phoebe.

"They'll be gathering up the stray wool caught on the brambles and bushes. What the wind sifts and the moors gather belongs to the poor here in Nantucket. They'll use all of it."

Clip—clip—clip—Father's shears worked fast on the thick woolly coats of the sheep Thomas held for him. Their soft, heavy coats fell off in one piece. Thomas carried them to the growing pile of wool on the sails.

"We can sit on it going home," said Lucretia. "This time we won't mind the bumps."

"How skinny the poor sheep look now!" said Phoebe, plucking handfuls of clover for them. "Will the wool grow back soon?"

"In no time," answered Thomas. "They're glad to get rid of it in this hot weather. Hurrah, only one more!" he shouted. He pushed a bleating ewe back into the fold. "Now for that brute Samson! He's the worst one of all!"

Samson hated to be held firmly by his horns while the big scissors traveled up and down his back, his stomach and his legs. He seemed to know what was in store for him. Each time Thomas tried to seize him, he ducked and ran around the fold. He frightened all the other sheep until they huddled together, bleating and trembling.

Lucretia, Phoebe and Sally danced with excitement. Each time the wicked old ram dodged out of the boy's reach. At first Father laughed, but he grew tired of waiting. Finally he vaulted over the fence of the pen to talk with a neighbor.

Then Lucretia had her bright idea.

She picked up the stick she had used before and waited till Samson had got himself to a corner. Then she thrust the stick through the fence and across the corner. "That will hem him in," she thought. "Now they can catch him and get him sheared without any trouble."

"Catch him quick now!" she yelled to her brother. By this time Thomas was both hot and exasperated. He didn't like to have Lucretia interfere, and he didn't move very fast.

The stick was not quite long enough to reach across the corner. Instead it hit the ram's flank. Samson kicked first, then butted his way through the flock. He knocked down part of the loosely built fence and raced off over the moor toward the merry-go-round.

"Now thee's done it," cried Thomas furiously. "Meddling as usual!"

Lucretia sat in the shelter beside the empty hampers. Mother, Sally, Father, Betsy, Phoebe and Thomas had gone off and left her. Samson had been caught finally, but not until he had upset a stand full of penny wares. It belonged to a peddler from the mainland. It had cost Father two dollars and seventeen pence to pay the damage for the broken wares.

122

While the rest of the family went to the clambake on the beach, Lucretia could sit quietly and
think, Father said. This would help her remember what unhappy results came of not minding
her own business. It would teach her also the
wisdom of holding her tongue.

Mother had given her two slices of plain bread and a cup of spring water. Lucretia could hear the laughter and shouts of the people at the clambake. She could see the pink light from the bonfire. But she didn't care. She could not have swallowed even a juicy clam dipped in hot butter. Disappointment lay like a hard stone inside her. Would she ever learn to control her anger?

She had spoiled the beautiful shearing day she had talked so much about to Phoebe. Father would scarcely have punished her so severely, just for trying to help. Or for being a busybody. But when Thomas had called her a meddler, Lucretia had screamed at him: "I wish thee wasn't my brother! I hate thee!" For a moment hate had really been in her heart.

It had gone away now, like the waves that rushed up the ocean beach and slid back quickly. Oh, why hadn't she stood still and not opened her mouth until her anger had left her?

124

Lucretia buried her face in an old jacket of Father's in a corner of the tent. The sun went down and it grew dim inside the shelter. The sound of a little girl's sobbing ceased. Lucretia had cried herself to sleep.

She did not hear Thomas when he came in. He shook her awake, and spoke gruffly to hide his embarrassment. "Come on," he said. "Father gave me pennies to take Sally and Phoebe on the flying horses. Only we none of us wanted to if——" Thomas stuck there for a second. "If thee couldn't go too. I asked Father and he said 'yes.' Come on, and I'll take you over. It's really a lot of fun."

It was night when Thomas, Sally, Lucretia and Phoebe drove back to Nantucket village behind Father and Mother and Betsy. The wool in the tip-cart was springy and comfortable. They went slowly this time. Father and Thomas both walked and led the horse and pony.

The moon shed a pale light over the pond and the moors. The wild music of the fiddles playing for people to dance, the sound of singing and laughter, and the soft tinkle of sheep bells followed them for a long distance. The three girls strained their ears to hear the music as long as possible. Finally the last sounds were muted. But the stars went with them all the way home.

Outwitting
a Sailor

"A-B-C-D-E-F-G——" Betsy stopped and looked up at Lucretia. "It's your turn now," she said. "Pay attention."

They were making a song of the alphabet. On this stormy January day the two of them were glad to be in the warm kitchen. They sat close to the slow-burning peat fire.

A year and a half had passed since the happy shearingtime in early June. Now Father was on the sea again. His last letter had been written from the Straits of Magellan. He had stopped there to buy a cargo of sealskins. Then he had gone on to China.

At home there were changes. Betsy was almost four and no longer the baby of the family. Mother was busier than ever, taking care of a new little sister named Mary. Already Sally was as tall as Mother. At twelve she could handle the heavy iron spiders and kettles as easily as a grownup. She could take her turn at the big loom on which all the family homespun was woven. She was a skillful weaver.

"Sally is my strong right arm. And Lucretia has enough head on her shoulders for two," Mother used to say.

This was a family joke, for Lucretia did not grow fast. Everything about her was small except her forehead. It was unusually large for so little a girl. She could think very quickly too.

"She has the Folger brow," Grandfather Folger often told Mother. "Benjamin Franklin had it too. His mother, Abiah Folger, was a Nantucketer and a cousin of ours."

It was true that Lucretia's nine-year-old head was full of good sense. When Mother had to be away these days, it was Lucretia she trusted rather than Sally. She could let her take full charge of Betsy. She could let her wait on customers and give them the correct change when they came to trade.

"H-I-J-K-L-M-N-O-P," Lucretia sang for Betsy above the click of her knitting needles.

Today, except for the cheerful glow of the fire, the big kitchen was gloomy. It was chilly in the corners of the room. The light from the gray winter sky was dim. Sleet pricked the windowpanes. The wind roared in the chimney.

"Poor Sinbad," said Betsy, "he has to stay outdoors! He must be very cold!"

"He knows enough when it storms to perch under the woodshed roof. It's dry there and his feathers keep him warm. Wild creatures are happier outside," Lucretia told her.

"Hark!" she added. A pounding of the door knocker echoed through the house. "That must be Dinah Bountiful with her brooms. She always comes around on the tenth day of the month. Mother said to exchange three pennies' worth of tea for a broom."

Lucretia laid her knitting down and ran upstairs. Betsy followed. Her short legs took the high steps one at a time.

Lucretia pushed the bolt in the front door and opened it. "Walk in—" she started to say. Then she stopped in astonishment. This was not Dinah, the old Indian peddler. A rough-looking stranger stood on the stoop.

Lucretia had seen men like him before, around the harbor docks. He was one of those roving seamen whalers picked up in foreign ports. Sometimes they got stranded on Nantucket for weeks before they sailed away again on an outgoing ship. Soon others would take their place.

Nantucket housewives were careful to keep their doors locked whenever any of these men were known to be in the town. Children were warned to stay away from these seamen.

"You have sealskins for Meestair Josiah Stevens?" asked the man. He stumbled over the English words. "He—he send me to get."

Lucretia hesitated. The man's face, with its insolent black eyes, did not look honest. What should she do? Father had shipped these costly sealskins back from the Straits. They belonged to Mr. Stevens, a wealthy neighbor. Mother had charge of the skins until Mr. Stevens called for them. Lucretia was sure Mr. Stevens would not send anyone like this seaman for them.

Betsy clutched Lucretia's skirt. The child's fear reminded Lucretia they were alone in the house. Mother and Sally and little Mary had left for the day. They were to help with the weaving and candlemaking at Grandmother Folger's.

Thomas was on the south side of the island. A schooner had grounded on the shoals in yesterday's gale. Whenever there was a shipwreck Nantucket men and boys patrolled the beaches. Sometimes they had to rescue people. Sometimes they were needed to help save the cargo.

"It is strange Mr. Stevens did not tell us he was sending thee," Lucretia said to her caller. "Besides, he must have gone very early this morning to the wreck, with the other men."

The sailor shrugged his shoulders. "I make mistake. Mrs. Stevens—she send me." He quietly planted one foot against the door to keep it open.

The lie sharpened Lucretia's wits. She knew Mrs. Stevens had gone to visit relatives on the Continent. How could she get rid of this man who must know there was no one else in the house? Suddenly Lucretia knew how—if only Betsy did not give her away! Fortunately Betsy was too frightened to say anything.

"I'll get my grandfather, Captain Folger, if thee will wait," she said politely and put her hand on the door latch of the Great Room.

The man stared sharply at her. At first he didn't look as though he believed her. But she stared back so bravely that his fear got the better of him. With an oath he turned away abruptly. The instant his foot moved off the sill Lucretia slammed the door and bolted it.

When she and Betsy peered out the Great Room window he was running down Fair Street. Soon he was lost in the driving sleet.

"Was he a bad man?" asked Betsy anxiously.

Lucretia held the child close. Her own heart was pounding. "He's gone now," she said at last. "We won't think of him again."

The key to Mother's shop hung from a ribbon around her neck. Lucretia unlocked the door and looked in. It made her feel better to see the bundle of sealskins behind the counter.

Back in front of the kitchen fire, the two children tried to forget what had happened. Betsy loved to play school. She drew letters and numbers on Lucretia's slate. Her older sister knitted. The rest of the morning passed pleasantly until it was time to eat.

Then Lucretia poked some potatoes under the hot ashes. They waited till a rich odor filled the kitchen. Then Betsy was allowed to pull each potato out with a long-handled fork. They ate them hungrily with hot butter and mugs of milk.

"What shall we do now?" Betsy asked. Lucretia had rinsed their mugs and was putting them away on the shelf.

"Thee could have a lesson in knitting," said Lucretia. "After that I'll dust the shop. See, it has stopped storming. The sun is trying to shine. Maybe someone will come to trade."

While she was showing Betsy how to hold the knitting needles someone knocked.

"There, I thought so!" exclaimed Lucretia. Betsy looked frightened. "Never fear," she added, "we'll look out the window before we open the door this time."

All the same she was glad to see who stood on the stoop. This time it was Dinah Bountiful. They were not afraid of her, though she looked a good deal like a witch. Her beach-grass broomsticks were flung over her shoulder. The loose ends of the cotton kerchief on her head blew wildly in the wind.

How weather-beaten Dinah looked from walking over the moors! The cold had deepened the wrinkles in her homely Indian face. It might have been carved from a piece of driftwood. It looked, Lucretia thought, like some of the broken timber the sea cast up on Nantucket beaches.

"Mother wishes one of thy brooms," she said to Dinah Bountiful. "Betsy will take thee to the kitchen fire while I fetch the payment."

In Mother's shop Lucretia placed a canister of tea on the counter. She measured out three pennies' worth of tea with a little brass shovel. Next, she slipped the tea into a twist of paper. Then, when she had put everything carefully back in its place, she locked the shop again.

When Lucretia got back to the kitchen Dinah was sitting in Mother's stiff-backed rocker before the fire. She was telling Betsy the Indian legend of the beginning of Nantucket.

"Manshope—" Dinah made large motions to describe the god of her tribe—"he tall as the sky. Ocean no bigger than puddle to Manshope. He walk in and catchum whale like you catchum minnow." Dinah pretended to scoop a small fish with her hand. "Then he roastum whale over volcano. He eatum whale just as you eat little fish. Whale make just one meal for Manshope. Each time he gettum anudder whale and rostum. Afterward he smokum pipe."

At this point Dinah pulled a dirty pipe out of her skirt pocket. It was filled with dried corn silk. She plucked a blade of straw from her brooms and held it over the glowing peat. Then, to Lucretia's dismay, Dinah lighted the pipe.

Puff—puff—a horrid smell of burning corn silk filled the kitchen. Oh, dear, what would Mother say to this? Lucretia knew it would be impossible to get the smell out of the room.

"And then what happened?" Betsy squirmed impatiently.

But Dinah did not answer. Her brown Indian face looked more wooden than ever. She rocked and puffed, rocked and puffed. At last the corn silk was all used up. Dinah leaned forward and knocked her pipe on the hearthstone. She pointed to the tiny heap of ashes she had made.

"Manshope do same thing," said Dinah Bountiful. "He knock pipe ashes into ocean heap many times and make Nantucket Island."

The pleased cackle with which Dinah ended showed she had enjoyed her little story. Usually when she came to trade, housewives did not let her settle down for a smoke. This time there were only children about.

When Lucretia handed her the package of tea, for one broom, the old Indian woman grunted her thanks. But she did not budge from her warm seat by the fire.

"My goodness," thought Lucretia, "will she ever go? How can I get rid of her?"

"I'm sure Mrs. Worth on Trader's Lane wants a broom too," Lucretia hinted.

But Dinah Bountiful seemed to have shut her ears. Her eyes were closed too. The heat from the fire seemed to have put her to sleep. The odor from her pipe and the musty smell of her damp wooolen clothing grew stronger every minute. Lucretia knew it was time to act. Her mother would expect it.

Lucretia made a face at Betsy. Betsy buried her face in Lucretia's lap to smother her giggles.

"I'll wake Dinah by dropping something," Lucretia decided. But just as she reached for the heavy skillet that hung against the chimney, the door knocker thumped loudly once more.

Their unwelcome guest opened her eyes with a start. Suddenly she was wide-awake.

"Maybe it's Mother!" cried Betsy. From the way Dinah Bountiful got smartly to her feet, Lucretia knew she thought so too. The old Indian woman was at the door ready to leave in a moment. But Lucretia would not open the door again before she knew who was there.

When they looked out the window, however, there stood the Widow Mitchell. Her head and shoulders were wrapped in a shawl.

"Is thee all right, Lucretia?" she asked in a shrill, excited voice. She gave Dinah such a sharp glance that the old Indian walked away in a huff.

140

"I had better stay till thy mother gets home, Lucretia," went on Mrs. Mitchell. "I met a thieving sailor tramp on Main Street five minutes ago. He has come to this part of the village because the men are away. I thought I'd better come right over to see if you children were safe."

"He would have stolen the sealskins Father sent home———" Lucretia began, but she was interrupted by the widow.

"Sealskins!" Mrs. Mitchell pounced on the word. She did not wait to hear more. "Does thee know what thee is saying, child? Furs are a prideful luxury. Captain Coffin could be read out of Meeting for less!"

Lucretia was so angry she grew pink. How dare anyone accuse Father of breaking the Quaker rule of plain dress! The Widow Mitchell was a troublemaker. She often spread untruths because she was somewhat deaf and didn't catch all that was said.

"My father is doing no wrong! All the captains in the China trade exchange sealskins for goods. He was only doing a kindness by sending them home for a neighbor. Mr. Josiah Stevens is not a Quaker, and he has a right to trade in anythink he thinks is fit!"

Lucretia's voice rang so loudly it startled even herself. She wanted the Widow Mitchell to hear every word plainly. And she did. For a minute Mrs. Mitchell was too taken aback to speak.

"Thee has a bold tongue, Lucretia Coffin," she said at last. "Thy quick temper will get thee into trouble unless thee learns to control it." But that was all she said.

"She will tell Mother, and Father will hear of it, and I shan't be able to explain to him," thought Lucretia. "Mrs. Mitchell is right about my getting angry. Why can't I learn to think before I speak?" She felt miserable as she and Betsy followed the widow to the kitchen.

But nothing of the sort happened. After Mrs. Mitchell had had a cup of tea and some of Mother's cookies she seemed in much better humor. She listened to Lucretia's story of the sailor and approved of the way the little girl had made him believe Grandfather was there.

When Mother and Sally and the baby came home the Widow Mitchell said nothing about Lucretia's "bold tongue." Instead she told Mother how clever Lucretia had been to know the sailor was a thief and to fool him.

Thomas walked in soon afterward. "We got everyone off the boat and most of the cargo," he told them. "See what I've got, too." He showed them his pockets, stuffed with rough green pods.

They were peanuts, the schooner's captain had said. They grew in the Carolina states and were good to eat. Everyone on the beach had been told to help himself to this strange new food. Nantucket folk had not seen or tasted it before.

144

Gathered around the kitchen fire that evening, the Coffin family roasted the peanuts and munched the rich brown meat inside.

Mother said it was a pleasant way to end a day which had begun with storm and the threat of danger. A good deal had been saved by courage and presence of mind, indoors as well as on Nantucket beaches. Father would be glad to hear that Thomas had played a part in the rescue and that Lucretia had used her head.

No Word
From Father

On a First Day in January, two years later, Thomas, Sally and Lucretia sat in the Great Room. They were dressed in their Meeting-House clothes. Their hands were folded in their laps. Their eyes were fastened on the visitor Mother had brought home.

Mrs. Elizabeth Coggeshall was a well-known Quaker minister who had come to preach to the Quaker Society there. Someone told her that Captain Coffin had not been heard from for twelve months and more, and that his family feared he had been lost at sea. So she offered to hold a "sitting" for Mother and the children.

They were greatly in need of comfort. They could not help thinking of the many Nantucket men who had sailed away, to be lost at sea.

"If only she could tell us what has become of Father!" thought Lucretia. She sat there looking meek and respectful, as a Quaker girl must be before a minister of her faith. But inside she was rebellious and unhappy.

"I don't want to be preached at! I want to know that Father is alive!" Lucretia cried out silently. She would have said it out loud, but she held her tongue for Mother's sake. Mother was always silent herself these days. She tried not to show her grief.

"I have not come to raise false hopes. I wish only to strengthen your courage," Mrs. Coggeshall was saying quietly. Her face was kind and sensible. Her eyes rested thoughtfully on Lucretia. She seemed to see what was in the little girl's mind and to understand her feelings.

"Those who have crossed the border called 'death' do not return. But we can think of them as continuing a journey," she went on. "Just as we know a ship continues its course after it has crossed the horizon line and disappeared. Just as we do not fear for a bird whose flight carries it beyond our seeing, we need have no fear for those who have gone on ahead of us."

Lucretia was listening now, in spite of herself. How often she had watched the ships and the gulls leave Nantucket for distant, invisible lands! If it was that way with Father, if he had merely left on a never-to-be-ended journey, she could bear his going better.

"You cannot escape sorrow, any more than this island, surrounded by the ocean, can escape storm." Mrs. Coggeshall spoke reasonably. "The storm passes and the sun shines again. Sorrow passes too, and new joys will cross your path, if you let them."

"But if our path will not be Father's path, how can joy cross it?" asked Lucretia in a low voice. "How can we ever be happy without Father?"

Thomas and Sally leaned forward in amazement to stare at their sister. It was a bold thing for an eleven-year-old girl to contradict a speaker. It was even worse to interrupt a "sitting." What would their visitor say? They themselves would not have dared open their mouths.

"Now, child," said Elizabeth Coggeshall kindly, "thee has raised a question and thee has a right to an answer—if thy heart will receive it." She beckoned Lucretia to come closer to her.

Thomas and Sally sat back in their chairs. The minister was not angry.

"Joy is peace. It is contentment and it is always found within." The gentleness in Mrs. Coggeshall's voice was beginning to melt the hard ache in Lucretia. For the first time she met the preacher's keen but loving glance.

"Listen to thy own heart, child. It will guide thee to peace. When thee is tempted to be quick-tempered or when thy tongue is sharp, thee is very unhappy afterward. Is it not so, Lucretia?"

The little girl nodded. Tears filled her eyes. This was the last promise she had made Father. She would listen earnestly when she grew angry. She would stop and listen. She would heed the still small voice within her and do its bidding.

"And when thee has been patient," continued Mrs. Coggeshall, "and thoughtful of thy mother, thee feels at peace. When thee thinks more of helping thy brother and sisters and thy friends than of getting something for Lucretia, thee finds a great joy. No sorrow can keep that kind of happiness from crossing thy path."

Mrs. Coggeshall stood up. The "sitting" had come to a close. "I do not have to remind this family that Captain Coffin is a skillful seaman, resourceful and brave."

The Coffins nodded. None of them trusted themselves to speak.

"You say his last letter came a year ago," Mrs. Coggeshall continued. "It told how his ship had been seized unlawfully at a port in Chile. Doubtless he has asked for a settlement, and often it takes a long time to get justice. He may have had to return on foot across the Andes Mountains to reach the Atlantic Coast and take ship again for home. That journey back would last many, many months. It is too soon to give up." There was a calm strength in her voice. Somehow it gave them all fresh hope.

Weeks had gone by since the Quaker minister had paid them a visit. Still no letter nor any news of Father had reached Nantucket. The winter evenings by the fireside were no longer the same. The family used to spend them in games and storytelling. Now worry about Father hung like a cloud over all their efforts to be cheerful.

Often in the middle of talk Mother's busy hands dropped her sewing. Her eyes looked into the fire without really seeing it. The children knew her thoughts were far off. They were with Father on his long journey home.

To comfort her Lucretia would draw her chair close to Mother's. After a while Mother would notice her and come back from her thoughts to the children's talk.

Thomas had left school to be an apprentice in Mr. Coleman's candle factory. He was seventeen now and old enough to be the main support of the family.

As the months dragged on and Father did not come back they all began to think about earning money. Sally stopped going to school because of the expense.

"I'm glad," she told Lucretia. "No more studying! Now I shall start weaving and tatting and selling my handiwork."

"Lucretia must go on with her education," Grandfather Folger said firmly at one family council. "For a Quaker girl there is no better way to make a living than by teaching."

"Poor thee!" whispered Sally. She felt sorry for anyone who had to study. But Lucretia's eyes shone with eagerness. She had been afraid Mother and Grandfather would take her out of school too. Now she could go on learning.

The April winds blew warmly over Nantucket that year. It was a happy month—a month when ships and sailors came home from distant lands. How everyone hoped that Father might come!

One day Sally, Thomas, Lucretia and Mother were eating their noonday meal when they heard the town crier's call. A ship had been sighted on the horizon!

Mother rose hastily from the table. "Quick, Lucretia, fetch the spyglass from the Great Room! I hope you have taken care of it."

The whole family hurried to the attic. Sally helped Betsy. Mother carried Mary up the three flights of stairs. Thomas rushed ahead to open the trap door to the widow's walk. Lucretia came running with the spyglass. She was glad that she had dusted it every day.

"It is just possible—" Mother tried to speak calmly—"that Father might be a passenger on someone else's ship. Of course it wouldn't have to be this ship. But if he is on it he will fly a signal to let us know."

Thomas had unlocked the trap door. Already he was on the walk. Mother followed him quickly. Then Sally and Lucretia climbed up with Betsy and Mary.

Mother's hands shook as she pointed the spyglass toward the ocean. She peered through it a long time. The children waited anxiously. What was it Mother saw? Lucretia's eyes could make out only a black spot on the horizon.

154

"I don't seem to be able to focus the glass right," Mother said at last. Her voice trembled. "Or else—or else there is no signal. Thee try, Thomas." She handed him the spyglass.

Thomas took it. Then Mother did a strange thing. She walked a step away and covered her face with her hands.

Sally and Lucretia looked at each other. Mother was crying. The children had never seen their mother cry before.

Betsy and Mary thought everyone had come to the walk for fun. They began to laugh and play. They liked the widow's walk.

"Hush!" Lucretia drew them as far from Mother as she could.

"Let them enjoy themselves," Mother said, rousing herself and smiling at her children. "Of course there was no reason to expect your father to be on this particular ship. Other ships will be coming to Nantucket."

"There is no signal," Thomas said finally. He lowered the spyglass.

No one said anything. Mary did not want Lucretia to hold her hand. She began to whimper and pull away.

Mother turned around then. "Come, we'll go down now, children." It was just as though she hadn't hoped Father would be on this boat, just as though she knew he would be on the next boat.

Lucretia drew a deep breath. Mother was all right again.

Journey's End

LATER IN THE day Lucretia and Sally were sitting in a sunny corner of the yard. Sally had brought the spinning wheel outside. She was spinning the carded wool into long strands and winding the strands into balls. The big family mending basket stood beside Lucretia. She was darning and patching. Betsy and Mary played near by with their dolls.

"I wish Mother would sit with us out here." Sally's foot tapped the treadle and the treadle made the wheel spin. "It would be good for her to be outside the house for a while. The sunshine would cheer her up."

Lucretia wove her darning needle in and out of the heel of Thomas' stocking before she answered. She remembered that Mother had said to her once: "Industry eases heartache. Let thee never forget that, Lucretia."

"Mother is sitting at her loom now because it comforts her to work."

Sally nodded gravely. "Work is an old Nantucket cure for sorrow. I'll tell thee one thing though, Lucretia," she went on. "I have made up my mind never to marry a sailor. If Father had owned a candle factory, or even if he had been a plain cooper, making barrels for the whalers, we would be much happier now."

But Lucretia wasn't listening. Her thoughts were in the loom room with Mother. The sound of the shuttle had stopped. Did Mother need comforting?

Lucretia gathered up her mending. "I'll take my darning inside for a while," she told Sally.

And it was then, just as Lucretia started for the house, that the event they had prayed for and waited for, so long, came to pass. No one was ever able to remember afterward who recognized Father first.

Mother was coming out of the kitchen. She held the length of linen she had finished weaving. At that very moment a man leaped over the picket fence into the yard.

He had no hat. The rough sailor's jacket he wore was ragged and stained. His boots were cracked and patched. The wind in his hair gave him a wild look. He stood there without a word, gazing at them.

Mother, Sally and Lucretia stared back. Betsy and Mary dropped their dolls.

"Who is it?" Lucretia's heart leaped at her own question.

Mother's face had grown white. She did not stir. Only her lips moved.

160

"Thomas!" she whispered.

"Anna—Sally—Lucretia—don't you know me?" Crying out their names, the man stepped forward. He caught Mother as she stumbled into his arms.

Father had come home!

How happy they were around the supper table that evening! Father had a long tale to tell them. It was full of misfortunes, to be sure, but full of interest and adventure too.

"The ship you saw this morning flew no signal because I was not on it," Father said. "The ship I boarded in South America went direct to Boston. I had no chance to let thee know what had happened. As soon as I reached Boston I came to Nantucket by the next packet."

"Sally has spun nearly enough wool to weave the clothes thee needs," Mother said.

"No wonder thee thought me a castaway, Anna." Father glanced down at his jacket and boots. "I hardly look like the captain of one of our Nantucket ships."

"We can listen to the stories of thy adventures as long as thee can stay home," Lucretia said contentedly. "But what happened to all the clothes thee had, Father?"

He laughed. "It was the long journey over the Andes that wore out my clothes. Once I got to the coast of Brazil, I took passage immediately for the United States. The ship's captain fitted me out with rough clothing for the voyage."

"It is well thee bought nothing," Mother assured him. "All thy Meeting-House clothes are safely stored in the attic. The girls and I will soon make thee fresh supplies. Now that the "Trial" is lost we shall need to save money, so thee can get a new ship. We will all work together. Sally does such fine handiwork that it sells very well on the mainland. Mr. Coleman says that Thomas is already one of his best workers. Lucretia will soon be a teacher."

"Perhaps there'll be no new ship. We must talk it over, Anna. Thee has suffered much, and I cannot risk another boat in the China trade. It is hard for Americans to get justice in South American courts."

"Would thee go into candlemaking, Father, like Mr. Coleman?" Sally asked eagerly.

"I know something of the trade myself now, sir." Thomas spoke up like the man he had become. "I could work with thee."

"Does thee really mean to give up the sea?" Mother's voice sounded as though it were too good to be true.

"Will thee stay home with us always, Father?" Lucretia put in. "Oh, say thee will!"

"There, there!" Father laughed. "What a lot of questions! It would mean leaving Nantucket and going to the Continent where there are more chances to make a living. We cannot decide hastily on so great a change."

The Mainlanders

AFTER CONSIDERING the matter carefully for several weeks the Coffin family had decided to make the change. On a warm July morning a crowd of friends had gathered on the Nantucket dock to wish them well. Captain Bunker's packet, the "Seabird," lay waiting for the tide to float her over the sand bar outside the harbor.

Her decks were heavily loaded. There were hampers of food, chests of linen, barrels of household utensils, horsehair trunks and furniture. They belonged to Captain Coffin. But he was "Captain" no longer. He and his family were leaving Nantucket for good.

"Keep an eye out for Sinbad, just for old times' sake," Thomas begged David Coleman. "Only a bad storm drives him into our woodshed now. Let me know if thee sees him." Thomas handed his friend a paper with his address on the Continent. "Be sure to write me about what thee is doing and what is going on in Nantucket. Whenever thee comes to Boston, be sure to come to see us. I shall miss thee."

"Write to me, Phoebe." Lucretia kissed her friend good-by. "I'll think of thee often when I am in the public school in Boston. I'll wish thee were sitting beside me."

"Why, Lucretia, isn't thee going to Quaker school there?"

"Father wishes us to go to the free schools on the Continent. He says he wants his children to be good mixers."

"How I shall miss thee, Lucretia! What wonderful new sights thee will see in the big city!"

"But we will always be Islanders, Phoebe! If we weren't so thankful that Father came home and isn't going to sea again, we couldn't bear to leave Nantucket!"

Captain Bunker made a trumpet of his hands. "All ashore!" he bellowed. His men had started to hoist the topsails of the "Seabird." They were casting off the straining lines which held the packet to the dock.

"Good-by, Phoebe! Good-by, Widow Mitchell! Good-by, Grandmother . . . Grandfather . . . Uncle William . . . Cousin Macy . . ."

Lucretia stood on the stern deck of the "Seabird" and waved her handkerchief. She was glad the wide brim of her poke bonnet hid her tears. The people she loved grew smaller and smaller on shore. She felt very small and alone, and Boston seemed very large and unfriendly at that moment. She wished she could remain in Nantucket.

The little town of Nantucket with its gray houses, its church steeples and its white Quaker Meeting House faded in the distance. Finally it vanished under the horizon. Only the island gulls followed the "Seabird" far out into the ocean.

At last they too were ready to say good-by. "Come back someday . . . come back!" Their lonesome call floated on the wind as they wheeled and flew back to Nantucket.

Lucretia's quill pen squeaked across the page as she wrote, making neat letters:

Dear Phoebe,

So much has happened, I have not had time to write thee for a long time.

I am no longer in Boston town but at Nine Partners, a town in New York State.

It is almost two years since we left Nantucket, but the Continent still seems like a foreign land. The rivers and lakes and harbors only make me homesick for the wide ocean. There are beautiful trees and forests, but I would rather look over an empty moor.

Customs on the Continent are very different from our Nantucket way. Even Father did not know how different.

Betsy and I went to the free schools, but the girls there have only two hours of school. They have to wait until the boys are let out.

In Boston they think it is improper for girls to learn geography! None of them can read a compass. In Boston they say female minds can hold only a little reading, writing and a few sums. Did thee ever hear such twaddle?

Father said very soon that Betsy and I must go back to Quaker schools. So here we are in a Friends' boarding school.

The rules here at Nine Partners are stricter than in Nantucket. The boys live at one end of our long schoolhouse, and we girls at the other end. We have separate classes and separate playgrounds. Even brothers and sisters cannot speak to each other except on First Days in the Common Room. It took us many days to travel here by coach from Boston. Betsy and I can't go home for two years!

I have made one true friend here. Her name is Sarah Mott. But, even so, friends from Nantucket are the oldest and best.

Pray write soon. I long for news of the Island.

Thy faithful friend, Lucretia.

"Did thee know how grave thy offense is, Lucretia? Doesn't thee know a girl must not enter the boys' part of the school?" It was Miss Susan Marriott who asked the questions. Her pleasant face was framed in a white Quaker cap. She looked shocked and surprised rather than angry.

Lucretia had been "sent for." She was in the Principal's office, where every pupil dreaded to go. She sat very primly, as she had been taught in Quaker school. Her hands were folded in her lap and her feet were crossed. But her feet did not touch the floor, although she was now fourteen. She was still small for her age.

"I did know," Lucretia answered quickly and honestly. "I went just the same."

"Furthermore," Miss Marriott went on more sternly, "I am told thee stole bread and butter from the table. Thee passed it under the door to a lad who was being punished for breaking a rule. What has thee to say to that?"

170

"I did not steal!" Lucretia's eyes burned. "If Master Brown said I did, he told an untruth. I gave Adam my own share of bread and butter because I knew he was hungry. I slipped it in my dress pocket at meal time."

"We shall suppose that Master Brown was mistaken." Miss Marriott glanced out the window to hide a twinkle in her eyes. So small, so outspoken a pupil was hard to scold. Miss Marriott was a courageous person herself, and she liked to see courage in her pupils.

"Thee reasons very well in thy lessons, Lucretia." Miss Marriott looked straight at her. Now her eyes were cool. "Will thee tell me why thee took the part of a pupil who misbehaved?"

"Because the way he was treated was unfair!" Lucretia burst out.

"Unfair that Adam should be punished?" Miss Marriott raised her eyebrows. "Do you think unruly pupils should not be punished?"

"Master Brown locked Adam in a dark closet the whole day and put him on dry bread and water, just because he whispered in class. That was a big punishment for a little fault. Teachers should be fair," Lucretia insisted, "and Master Brown is not fair."

"If Master Brown was unfair to Adam, Adam should tell me about it himself," Miss Marriott said firmly. "Thee does not have to look out for Adam or any of the other boys. Now thee must be punished too, Lucretia. I cannot allow thee to break our strictest rule. Thee will be forbidden to go to the playground for a month. I consider that a very light punishment."

"Miss Marriott——" Lucretia hesitated.

"Well? Thee is trying my patience, Lucretia. I have let thee off lightly. Girls should be dismissed from school for entering the boys' quarters." The Principal stood up as though there were no more to be said.

172

Lucretia's dark eyes flashed. "I do not mind for myself. I only wanted to say that there has been unfairness before, and Adam and the others will not speak about it. They are afraid."

"Afraid of whom and of what?" asked Miss Marriott sharply.

"Afraid of thee. They are afraid they will be punished twice as hard for complaining about a teacher. They dare not speak out."

There was a long silence. Miss Marriott's face had grown red. Her Quaker pride was touched. Quaker rules were supposed to be just and fair. Did she need to be reminded by a child?

"Fear is not one of thy failings at least, Lucretia," she said finally. Her voice was not unkind. "Thee has a right to say what thee thinks. Thee may go now."

"She didn't ask me to say I was sorry when I couldn't say it," thought Lucretia, as she left the Principal's office. "She is fair, after all."

174

Lucretia was forbidden the playground. But Sarah Mott proved herself a true friend indeed. She kept Lucretia company. She would not join in any games until Lucretia could play also. Adam, the boy Lucretia had helped, was Sarah Mott's cousin.

One day the two girls were sitting together, sewing. "Does thee think thy parents would let thee visit me this summer?" asked Sarah. "Mother says I may bring home a friend. Oh, Lucretia, my family—especially my brother James—will love thee," Sarah said, smiling.

"Is James so funny?" asked Lucretia.

"He is a dear," Sarah said. "He's a great giant of a boy with sandy hair and blue eyes, and he has the softest heart in the world. But James is terrified of girls. He is tongue-tied with them."

"Poor James." Lucretia laughed. "I shall like him just the same—if he is as nice as thee. And I shall dearly love to visit thy family."

That summer Lucretia went to the Motts'
home in the country near New York City. Sarah
was surprised that Lucretia and James got along
so well together. James was shy, and often he
was silent. But his smile was full of friendly
understanding. Soon Lucretia felt she had
known him all her life.

When James looked into Lucretia's bright
eyes he forgot he was afraid of girls. He even
found his tongue.

Dear Friend
James

AFTER TWO years at Nine Partners School, Lucretia and Betsy went home for a visit. The Coffin family had moved from Boston to Philadelphia. Father had a new business there. The girls could hardly wait to see the new house and a new little sister named Martha. It was a happy visit, but it lasted only two weeks.

Then she and Betsy went back to school. But now Lucretia was no longer a pupil. Miss Marriott asked her to be an assistant teacher. This made Lucretia very happy. She had always wanted to teach. There was another nice surprise. James Mott was a new schoolmaster!

177

One First Day Lucretia and Betsy were strolling arm in arm on the school grounds. Their time at Nine Partners was nearly over.

"Miss Marriott says she will make me a regular teacher if we stay one more year," Lucretia told Betsy. "She will pay me a salary. And she will give thee thy schooling free."

"Oh, Lucretia, it is because thee has done so well!" cried Betsy proudly. "Did thee say yes?"

Lucretia smiled and shook her head. "We must get Father's consent first. I have no close friend here now that Sarah Mott has left. Still, I'll be happy to stay if thee wants to."

"But thee has a close friend here. Surely thee knows who!" Betty said mischievously.

"I hope no one has been talking nonsense to thee." Lucretia looked at Betsy severely.

"No one," Betsy said quickly. "But I can't help noticing James would rather talk to thee than anyone else in school."

"James just happens to know me better than other people here. That's because of my visit to Sarah. James is bashful and he finds teaching a trial. It is a pity," said Lucretia, "for he is a fine teacher and a well-loved master."

"Thee likes him too—isn't it so, Lucretia?" Betsy's eyes twinkled with fun.

During the next year at Nine Partners Lucretia and James talked about many things together. She and James thought alike about everything that mattered. They both wanted to be good Quakers and good Americans. They both wanted to make the world better.

At Nine Partners all the teachers talked about world affairs. Everyone hoped the country's new President, James Madison, would be a wise leader. They did not want to see America at war, as Europe was. They asked themselves if people in a free country ought to own slaves. They asked what they could do to fight oppression.

"We Quakers believe that everyone who works should receive a just wage," declared Miss Marriott. "Quakers believe that our Heavenly Father loves all His children alike. How then can we believe He made some of His children free, and some to be slaves?"

"There is much injustice in the world," said young James Mott. "Some nations are unfair to others. Some persons are unfair. They take advantage of the people who work for them—men and women both. What can Quakers do about this? How can we improve conditions?"

"We can set a good example," replied one of the teachers. "We can do right ourselves."

"Yes," added Miss Marriott, "Quakers do not believe in fighting those with whom they cannot agree. But they do believe in coming to the aid of all who are wronged or oppressed. That is our way of fighting injustice. We believe it will be more effective than going to war."

So Lucretia and James decided they wanted to be soldiers in the peace-loving Quaker way.

"To speak out honestly for truth and to defend the weak take bravery. It needs as much courage as fighting with guns," said Miss Marriott.

Many things took bravery, James knew. Long before he found the courage to tell her, he was in love with Lucretia. She was quick-witted, lively and gay. She had a fiery courage. But how could she ever admire anyone as quiet and unexciting as he was?

At the same time Lucretia was thinking that though James was shy and quiet, he was also wise and loyal. His friendship never wore out. It was always there to lean on. So was his courage. She realized that no one—not even Sarah Mott—could ever be so close and dear a friend as James. And now it was time to say good-by to him and to everyone at Nine Partners! It was time to go home to Philadelphia.

The Nantucket Way

"LUCRETIA COFFIN, what *is* the matter with thee?" Lucretia was giving herself a good scolding. She closed the house door and set off down the cobbled street. "When thee was at school thee wished thee was home. Now thee is in Philadelphia and thee keeps wishing thee was at Nine Partners!"

Even the family had begun to notice that something was wrong.

"Moping, Lucretia?" Sally had teased this morning. "That's a sign of love."

"Lucretia feels homesick for Nine Partners, of course," Mother interrupted quickly. "Now if thee will do some errands for me, Lucretia, I could finish Martha's dress. Thee could make thyself useful. And at the same time thee could see more of Philadelphia."

But Lucretia hardly saw Philadelphia at all, though she went to every place on Mother's list. Her mind was full of something else. While she walked to the butcher's she kept thinking, "Everyone at Nine Partners has written me a letter except James."

Next she went to the grocer's. There she remembered that James had once said, "Words come hard to me. I'd rather saw wood than write a letter."

On the way to the draper's she decided sadly, "I shall never hear from James. He'll soon make other friends. Out of sight is out of mind."

By the time she reached home Lucretia was feeling very sorry for herself. She had to stop and fumble in her pocket for a handkerchief.

"I shall certainly *not* write to James," she made up her mind for the hundredth time. Hastily she dabbed at her eyes.

She dried them just in time. Betsy opened the door suddenly. Her face was bright with excitement. "Well," she cried, "guess who's here!"

Then she blurted out the news. "James Mott arrived while thee was gone. He's left Nine Partners for good. He says he wants to be a businessman in Philadelphia!"

"Did thee say *James?*" Lucretia was so astonished she dropped one of her bundles. Mother's soup greens spilled all over the floor.

"Father told James he needed a clerk in his office. Mother said he could stay in the room on our top floor!" Betsy rattled on. She stooped to pick up carrots and onions.

"My goodness!" Lucretia laughed joyfully. She dumped the rest of her packages on a chair. She whipped off her bonnet and patted her hair.

"Do I look all right?" she asked.

But before Betsy could answer she ran to the parlor door and opened it. There stood James. He was as tall, awkward and tongue-tied as ever. But his honest eyes told Lucretia all she had longed to read in a letter.

Lucretia was eighteen and James twenty-one when they stood up together in the Quaker Meeting House on Pine Street in Philadelphia to become man and wife. Lucretia wore a plain gray Quaker dress and bonnet, but no bride ever looked more charming.

Although she lived the rest of her life on the mainland, Lucretia did not forget her island home. She went back whenever she could to visit her relatives and her old school friend, Phoebe Worth. She was eighty-three when she visited Nantucket for the last time.

"Dear Lucretia, how glad I am to see thee!" Phoebe hugged her friend. She had come down

to the wharf to greet her. "If only James were here, our happiness would be complete."

"It comforts me, Phoebe, to come back here," said Lucretia. "Since James died I am more homesick than ever for Nantucket."

"And yet thee has so many friends on the mainland and abroad. The help thee has given wronged and unhappy people has made thee famous, Lucretia."

"Without James," answered Lucretia, "I could have done little. For women are not respected on the mainland as they should be, Phoebe. James and I fought to free them, as well as the poor slaves. But there is still much to be done. Women have not the legal rights to which all human beings are entitled."

"Thee must tell us more about it tomorrow, Lucretia. Everyone is coming to Abigail's fireside 'conversation.' We know thee loves our old Nantucket customs."

The next day the Great Room of Cousin Abigail Folger's house was filled with people. They sat in a large circle around the bright flames in the fireplace. Lucretia had the seat of honor in the center. She looked very happy. Her face was beautiful in old age. Loving service for others had made it so. Her dark eyes glowed with affection for her Nantucket friends.

There, across the room, sat David Coleman, Thomas' old playmate. His hair was quite white now. He smiled at her. "We used to call thee 'spitfire,' Lucretia, but now we wouldn't dare! Thee has become a great Quaker preacher."

"What a time I had with that bold tongue of mine!" Lucretia laughed.

"Oh, but thee has needed it in thy preaching," David reminded her. "How else could thee speak out against evil and defend the right?"

"The Elders made thee a preacher when thee was very young," Phoebe said proudly.

"Yes, I was twenty-five," answered Lucretia. "My little son had just died, and I turned very earnestly to God for comfort. I listened to the Inner Voice. I began to speak in Meeting of the light which came to me. Those days seemed dark, but I can see now that God was preparing me for my life work."

"Many honors have come to thee, Lucretia," said a friend. "Why haven't they changed thee? Other islanders have left us for the mainland. When they return they seem like strangers. But thee is different. Thee is still one of us."

"I suppose it's because I love Nantucket better the longer I live away from it," Lucretia said. "In a big world full of different types of people, the strong rule and the weak often suffer cruelty and injustice. The settlers on this little island were able to make a kinder, freer way of life. They weren't bound by the customs of the mainland."

190

"It's true our island was far out at sea," agreed Abigail Folger. "We had to govern ourselves."

"Nantucket women had to be more independent than women on the mainland," Lucretia went on. "Their husbands were often away for years on long sea voyages. The wives and mothers left behind had to do men's work as well as their own. So Nantucket women became strong, capable and brave."

"And sometimes ships were lost at sea. Then the women had to earn a living for their families," Phoebe added.

"That almost happened to my mother," Lucretia reminded them. "But fortunately Father came home after all. I shall never forget his homecoming, and how my mother wept for joy!"

"Yes, thy mother kept a shop and she traded on the Continent while thy father was at sea," Abigail Folger remembered. "Everyone praised her good business head."

"Nantucket women were better educated than their mainland sisters," put in David Coleman.

"That is because we Islanders were mostly Quakers," Lucretia pointed out. "We believed that all His children are equal in God's sight. So in Nantucket women were given the same opportunities as men. In many parts of the world women are oppressed by unfair laws."

"Thee has stayed loyal to our Nantucket ideals. That's why we love thee," declared Phoebe.

"Why, how could I forget the Nantucket way of life? I was brought up in it," exclaimed Lucretia. "It made me want to help all the enslaved and suffering people in the world. How often I have wished they might have the peace and freedom we know here!"

More About This Book

WHEN LUCRETIA MOTT LIVED

1793 LUCRETIA COFFIN WAS BORN ON NANTUCKET ISLAND, MASSACHUSETTS, JANUARY 3.

There were fifteen states in the Union.

George Washington was President, 1789-1797.

The population of the country was about 3,930,000.

1804 THE COFFIN FAMILY MOVED TO BOSTON AND LATER TO PHILADELPHIA.

Lewis and Clark explored the Northwest, 1804-1806.

Zebulon Pike explored the area now known as Kansas, Colorado, and New Mexico, 1806.

Robert Fulton built the "Clermont," first practical steamboat, 1807.

1811 LUCRETIA MARRIED JAMES MOTT.

The War of 1812 was fought, 1812-1815.

"The Star-Spangled Banner" was written, 1814.

The first steam-powered warship was launched in New York Harbor, 1814.

1817   LUCRETIA MOTT BECAME A TEACHER, BUT LATER GAVE UP TEACHING TO BECOME A MINISTER.

Florida was purchased from Spain, 1819.

The Monroe Doctrine was issued, 1823.

Peter Cooper built the first steam locomotive in the United States, 1830.

1833   LUCRETIA MOTT HELPED TO FOUND THE AMERICAN ANTI-SLAVERY SOCIETY.

Samuel Morse invented the telegraph, 1835.

American settlers reached Oregon, 1836.

The Iowa Territory was formed, 1838.

1840   LUCRETIA MOTT HELPED TO ORGANIZE THE FIRST WOMEN'S RIGHTS CONVENTION.

The Mexican War was fought, 1846-1848.

Harriet Beecher Stowe's book *Uncle Tom's Cabin* was published, 1852.

The War between the States was fought, 1861-1865.

The Thirteenth Amendment to the Constitution, forbidding slavery, was ratified, 1865.

194

1880   LUCRETIA MOTT DIED NEAR PHILADELPHIA,
       PENNSYLVANIA, NOVEMBER 11.

Rutherford B. Hayes was President.

There were thirty-eight states in the Union.

The population of the country was about 50,155,000.

DO YOU REMEMBER?

1. What was Nantucket Island like when Lucretia Coffin lived there as a girl?

2. What work did Mrs. Coffin do and how did Lucretia help her?

3. How did Lucretia and Thomas obtain the tern Sinbad for a pet?

4. What kind of clothing did Lucretia help to knit for the family?

5. How did the people work to put out the fire in Nathan Brown's woodpile?

6. How did Lucretia and Phoebe try to protect the Coffin house from the fire?

7. What presents did Captain Coffin bring home to his family?

8. What happened at sheep shearing time on Nantucket Island?

9. How did Lucretia get rid of the sailor tramp who came to the door?

10. What problem did Lucretia have with the old Indian peddler, Dinah Bountiful?

11. Why did the Quaker minister, Mrs. Elizabeth Coggeshall, come to the Coffin home?

12. Where did the Coffin family decide to move after Captain Coffin came home?

13. Where did Lucretia go away to school shortly after the family moved?

14. How did Lucretia happen to become a teacher?

15. Whom did Lucretia marry?

16. What story did Mrs. Mott, as an old lady, tell her old friend Phoebe?

IT'S FUN TO LOOK UP THESE THINGS

1. What is Nantucket Island like today, and what products are grown there?

2. What famous book did Harriet Beecher Stowe write to help the anti-slavery movement?

3. What was meant by the women's rights movement, which Lucretia Mott helped to start?

4. When did woman suffrage finally go into effect in this country?

5. What other causes besides anti-slavery and women's rights did Lucretia Mott support?

6. Where did Lucretia Mott live during the later years of her life?

INTERESTING THINGS YOU CAN DO

1. Collect pictures to show how people dressed when Lucretia Coffin was a girl?

2. Draw a map to show the location of Nantucket Island off the coast of New England.

3. Make a list of other prominent persons who supported the anti-slavery cause.

4. Prepare a report on the Emancipation Proclamation to read to the class.

5. Find out how woman suffrage was adopted in this country and give a report.

6. Name a few women who have held important offices since woman suffrage was approved.

OTHER BOOKS YOU MAY ENJOY READING

America Grows Up, Gerald W. Johnson. William Morrow.

Becky and Her Brave Cat Bluegrass, Miriam Mason. Macmillan.

Clara Barton: Girl Nurse, Augusta Stevenson. Trade and School Editions, Bobbs-Merrill.

Flagship Hope, The, Aaron Lopez, Lloyd Alexander. Farrar.

Heroines of the Early West, Nancy Wilson Ross. Random.

Railroad to Freedom, Hildegarde H. Swift. Harcourt.

INTERESTING WORDS IN THIS BOOK

apprentice (ă prĕn′tĭs) : young person, who by agreement serves another person for a period of time in order to learn an art or trade

astonished (ăs tŏn′ĭshd) : surprised, amazed

bonnet (bŏn′ĕt) : kind of hood with strings for tying under the chin

chantey (shàn′tĭ) : song sung by sailors in rhythm with their work

compass (kŭm′pȧs) : instrument for showing directions, consisting of a needle that points to the north magnetic pole

contradict (kŏn′trȧ dĭkt′) : deny the truth of

cooper (koop′ēr) : person who makes or repairs barrels, casks, buckets, and other containers made of wood

ember (ĕm′bēr) : glowing piece of fuel burning in a fire

gangplank (găng′plăngk′) : movable, bridge-like platform used for boarding or leaving a ship

greedy (grēd′ĭ) : having a keen appetite, ravenous, covetous

hoist: raise

homespun (hōm′spŭn′) : cloth made of yarn which has been prepared at home

horizon (hȯ rī′z′n) : line where the earth and sky seem to meet

hummock (hŭm′ŭk) : small, rounded hill

meddler (mĕd′lēr) : person who busies himself with other people's affairs

oppression (ŏ prĕsh′ŭn) : cruel or unjust treatment

peat (pēt) : special kind of soil used for fuel

peddler (pĕd′lẽr) : person who travels about with wares for sale

pewter (pū′tẽr) : mixture of copper and tin used for making tableware

porridge (pŏr′ĭj) : broth made of ground cereal boiled in water or milk

resourceful (rẻ sōrs′fo͞ol) : good at thinking of things to do

spermaceti (spûr′má sē′tĭ) : waxy solid made from the oil of the sperm whale, used especially in making candles

spyglass (spī′glȧs′) : small telescope used for making distant objects appear nearer and larger

starboard (stär′bōrd) : right side of a ship to a person facing the bow

telescope (tĕl′ẻ skōp) : instrument used for making distant objects appear nearer and larger

warned (wôrnd) : cautioned, admonished

whale (hwāl) : large air-breathing mammal that lives in the ocean

wharf (hwôrf) : platform used for loading and unloading ships

whittle (hwĭt′′l) : pare or cut shavings from wood, as with a knife

Childhood

OF FAMOUS AMERICANS

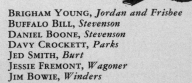